*Award-winning journalist **Declan Hassett** is a former Arts Editor of the* Irish Examiner *where he worked from 1962 to 2004. He was editor of the* Evening Echo *from 1976 to 1985.*

He edited the AIB Award winning book The Rockies *for the GAA Centenary Year in 1984. His three-volume memoir consisted of:* All Our Yesterdays, The Way We Were *and* Passing Through.

His play Up The Rebels *was commissioned by the Cork County Board to mark the millennium year in 2000. The world premiere of* Sisters *was at the Everyman Palace during Cork's tenure as European Capital Of Culture in 2005. It toured Ireland, went to Edinburgh Arts Festival and Anna Manahan's performance in* Sisters *earned her a prestigious Drama Desk nomination in the US. Declan Hassett's play* Survivors, *set in Civil War Ireland, premiered at the Cork Arts Theatre in 2006.*

MAKE 'EM LAUGH!
—— *A Golden Age of Theatre* ——

DECLAN HASSETT

The Collins Press

EVERYMAN
PALACE
THEATRE

Published in 2008 by
The Collins Press
West Link Park, Doughcloyne
Wilton, Cork
and
Everyman Palace Theatre
15 MacCurtain Street, Cork

British Library Cataloguing in Publication data

Hassett, Declan
    Make 'em laugh: a golden age of theatre
    1. Theater – Ireland – Cork – History – 20th century
    2. Theater – Ireland – Cork – History – Anecdotes
    I. Title II. Everyman Palace Theatre

    792'.0941956'0904

ISBN: 978-1905172849

Typesetting by TypeIT, Dublin
Typeset in Adobe Garmond
Printed in Ireland by ColourBooks Ltd.

Cover pictures
Front cover main picture: Michael Twomey and Frank Duggan of Cha
and Miah fame. For all other photos, please see the text.

Contents

Acknowledgments

Special thanks to the board of Thomas Crosbie Holdings and to Managing Director Anthony Dinan, for access to *Irish Examiner* and *Evening Echo* archives. Also special thanks to the Cork Opera House.

Particular thanks to Naomi Daly, Eimear O'Herlihy and Michael Twomey for their constant support for this project.

Original sources of photographs, when known, are acknowledged and sincere apologies for any oversight in this regard.

Introduction

When Dan Lowry opened his Palace of Varieties on King Street in Cork in 1897 little did he know that one hundred and twelve years later it would still be thriving as a centre for live performance. It is also doubtful if he appreciated at the time the impact that the thousands of variety performers he imported to appear at the Palace would have on the local populace. Not only were many generations of Cork audiences entertained but the experience of sitting in the Palace, or the old Opera House across the river, was the catalyst for many Corkonians to simply get up and do it themselves.

The personalities which the following pages celebrate come from a long line of performers threading its way through the twentieth century to the present day. But while pantomime thrives, other forms like the variety show and revue are virtually extinct in our televisual, IT age. So it is essential that we pause, take stock, acknowledge and salute an era in the history of our show business, populated with a cast of extraordinary larger than life characters who moved us, made us cry with laughter, and who revelled in simply reflecting us back to ourselves, warts and all.

I never had any hesitation when it came to selecting a writer for this book. I first got to know him when he was the innovative and hugely personable Arts Editor of the *Irish Examiner*. No matter how big or small the artistic endeavour, your first port of call was always Declan Hassett. And with his innate decency and generosity he would do his utmost to give coverage to your play or exhibition or poetry reading. At this stage, of course, he had a lifetime in journalism behind him, but to me he was an arts chronicler extraordinaire and entrusting him with this book was, as when he became a playwright on retiring from the *Examiner*, a natural progression.

Pat Talbot
Director, Everyman Palace Theatre

Preface

This book should have been written years ago. The story of Cork comedy theatre has begged, even deserved, to be told. Now, at last, the 'laughter years' ring from stage to page. Finally those who were part of that magical time, that golden era for theatre in Cork, remember with fondness those happy moments, not yet beyond recall.

These precious memories are now a matter of record because of the vision of Pat Talbot, Director of the Everyman Palace. He felt strongly that those who trod the boards, whether working backstage or front of house, should receive some form of recognition. This is their story – the story of a time when they were the star turns; when the all too fleeting spotlight was theirs. *Make 'Em Laugh!* is dedicated to those who have gone from us; and equally to those who are proud to remember them as brothers and sisters of the unique world of performance.

Pat Talbot told me of his consuming desire to capture that special period from the 1940s when it seemed that it was always 'show time'. He commissioned this book, with the support of the Everyman Palace Board, as the second in a series that opened with Vera Ryan's *Dan Donovan: An Everyman's Life* (The Collins Press, 2008).

I am not an historian, but I do have a sense of history. My own life has been enriched by those who have put on the powder and the paint. That tradition is being maintained to the present day as 'live' theatre battles for survival, while the nation and the world succumbs to the distractions of interminable soaps and reality TV, the modern equivalents of watching paint dry.

This book is not so much about 'the good olde days'; it is rather about the people who have raised our spirits and lifted us out of ourselves, just by being up there on the stage. Some of those were dolled-up men acting the panto dame, while others dressed up (or down) as loveable rogues, fairy godmothers, bungling barons, wicked witches, hardchaws, spivs, soft-touches, principal boys who were really girls, and even mighty mice pulling pumpkin carriages.

Step into the Barnum and Bailey world of suspended disbelief. Welcome to that forever-and-ever-land, larger than life, where we laugh and cry at spitting images, characters, caricatures, cronies perched on pub stools: this, the original and best transformer-world of kings and queens, handsome princes and sleeping beauties. Although you are not reading a definitive record of these times, you will be led on a journey through the mysterious realm of rehearsal venue, dressing room fever, backstage drama, the sweet, intoxicating anticipation of an opening curtain, and the collective gasp at a well-dressed set.

Meet the men and women who managed to keep the 'day job' while juggling the topsy-turvy world of getting to the backstage door, sandwich in one hand, wrong script in the other; late again as the director paces side-stage, wondering if all the effort would be worthwhile and if everything, once again, would come 'all right on the night'.

My brief for this book was to mark the contribution of those who gave up whole sections of their lives in their pursuit of the fine art of comedy theatre. A daunting task, but made easier by the fact that some of that theatre's finest practitioners continue to pace the boards or, if not, are blessed to recall happy hours when their names were up in lights, when their biog notes made for easy reading before lights came down, and there was that magic moment at another opening of another show.

I decided that this book should be less about the actual shows and more about the people who took a deep breath and entered stage right, hoping that the cue was really theirs and that there would be no unseemly collision centre stage. Were they in the right theatre on the right night? Could they be heard by the couple holding hands in the back row of the stalls, the crisp-crunchers in the gallery, the marshmallow maulers, the woman with the nervous cough? All of them unseen, somewhere out there in the darkness.

Armed then with biro, large notebook and tape recorder, I knocked on people's doors, drank countless cups of coffee and arrived back at my desk full of what I had heard as they reminded me of that night sixty, fifty, forty, thirty, twenty, even ten years ago, when a star was born and a show had soared – or died. That could have been the night that the critics got their name right, or did not notice the 'dry' when an entire play pivoted on a line – a word that would not come.

Welcome to the world of first-night nerves, of actors lost on tour; a world where players mount the stage in the wrong costume, stressed and dying with the flu. Outside it is midwinter darkness as the last cigarette is smoked at the backstage door before a dash to change in a crowded room. Who owns that pale face, looking back from gilt-framed mirror?

Then, the disembodied five-minute call; it is too late now for first-night nerves. Stage lights mimic a Caribbean sun while one's 'pretend' lover is flicking sand from polished, brown feet. Adonis speaks: 'I'm leaving you, darling'. You freeze dry, stammer, but it is too late as the interval curtain sweeps across. There is that dash upstairs for strong tea in a plastic cup as you wonder why you ever wanted to be an actor in the first place. Director sidles in, smiles weakly, whispers audibly: 'You were simply marvellous; pity about the dry . . . darling!'

It is this 'unreal' setting that bewitches players and public as art attempts to imitate life; the blurring, the coalescing of the two, the essence of this strange attraction to the world of live performance.

I have been the awestruck boy in the 'gods', the teenager in love with the leading lady, later the critic on a deadline for the next day's paper. I've known first-night nerves when my own work was seconds from curtain, and I faced the judgement of my peers.

Live theatre can be a trapeze act without the safety net, but the glorious uncertainty contrasts well with the sometimes numbing predictability of TV, and quite often, cinema.

Come with me then: rediscover the delights so generously created down the decades by the scriptwriters, directors, actors, designers, stage-managers, production crews, from front of house to stage door.

Comedy theatre is the chosen subject but, of necessity, and in the interest of the reader, I sometimes take a broader path in our search for the past. This record is not always in chronological order, but rather reflects the reminiscences of those being interviewed.

The sheer versatility of those involved meant they were able to slip seamlessly from one discipline to another and back again, quite often in the space of one season. It could be a work of high drama or low farce, scintillating satire, operetta, sparkling revue, or magical musical comedy. Opening night and the performance is all, no middle ground, no second chance, no going back, it lives or dies here – this is not a rehearsal.

Declan Hassett

Chapter 1
Stage-struck

Michael Twomey

Hard to imagine now that Michael Twomey, a doyen of Irish theatre, whose dulcet and measured tones grace theatre evenings and adjudication nights around the country, was thought once to have an 'appalling' accent.

Admittedly that was only his mother's view of the lad who grew up in the 1940s at Alverna Terrace on the Mardyke, beneath the elms. It was something of a theatrical commune. Neighbours included Der Breen, once manager of the Palace, director of the Cork Film Festival and, later, National Film Censor. In his memoir Dan Donovan recalls happy moments spent in the Breen household around that time. Another resident was Ted Healy, a prominent member of the Cork Shakespearean Company, and yet another was the tenor Myles McSwiney who made several broadcasts from the old Radio Éireann studios in the women's jail at Sunday's Well Road, Cork.

As a boy, Michael took the short stroll to Presentation College. He was a tall lad for his age and the school, which considered prowess in rugby as important as scholastic success, possibly saw in him a safe pair of hands. His potential as a lock-forward could, after all, lead to a secure and pensionable job on the Mall. As events unfolded, with art imitating life on the stage, that early promise was not far off the mark.

His mother, Kathleen, who in her single days was secretary to Sir Patrick Hennessy at Henry Ford Motor Assembly Plant on the Marina, had a dear friend, May Patterson. Michael recalls that she had a lovely cake shop on Washington Street. Kay and May were habitual first-nighters at the old Opera House and Michael was soon introduced to the heady world of pantos at Christmas, although he has few strong memories of those productions which meant so much to so many down the years. However, pantos were to become a major part of his stage life much later. His few early recollections include the metal steps which led to the 'gods' on the northern side of the old Opera House and the welcoming foyer at Emmet Place.

Mother Twomey was determined that her growing boy was going to learn to 'speak proper', as the Corkism goes. He was about to come under the influence of that theatrical giant, James Stack, teacher of drama at the Cork School of Music. And, given his mother's ambitions, it is hardly surprising that Michael appeared in his first play, Eugene O'Neill's *Ah, Wilderness!*, at the ripe old age of eleven.

> I played the son Tommy, with Lorna Daly, Lorraine Jones, Ignatius Comerford, Joe Lynch, Doris Pinker and Charlie McCarthy. That was 1944 and I was a pupil of Stack's from the age of eight.

My mother was one of Father O'Flynn's first pupils He was then the chaplain to Our Lady's Hospital on the Lee Road. He had rooms there from which he conducted Shakespearian classes. My mother played Ophelia in *Hamlet*, directed by Fr O'Flynn.

When a famous UK touring company came to Cork, they advertised for young actors and actresses and my mother sucessfully auditioned. Her parents, however, were adamant, unlike Mrs Worthington that their daughter would not appear on stage under any circumstances.

This incident in her own childhood may have coloured Kay Twomey's thinking. She was certain that her precious son Michael would not be 'Pres-ganged' onto the rugby playing fields. He was certainly not going to play for Ireland; she would rather he took to the stage, as indeed he did.

One can only conjecture what Mrs Twomey would have thought of Michael's lasting fame as Miah in the much-loved 'Cha and Miah' partnership, and his country cousin character, Paddy Joe Canavaun from Tooreendohenybeg. Sadly, by that period in his

Double Act – Cha (Frank Duggan) and Miah (Michael Twomey) with Cork's own Shandon steeple in the background.
(© Joe McCarthy)

career she had passed away. She could also have been impressed by Michael's association with the fertile era of Irish theatre during which John B. Keane and his plays took the country by storm, threatening the safe and conservative world that the Abbey Theatre represented.

This, however, is to get ahead of ourselves; back to Michael's early years in theatre. 'My father Jim was in the accountancy department in the City Hall. His particular interest was opera. He was a member of the North Cathedral Choir as was James Stack.'

Michael attended Father O'Flynn's Shakespeare classes, at The Loft – where incidentally he met his wife-to-be, Marie. 'It was there that I learned to appreciate Shakespeare. Above all, I learned the importance of interpretation, the art of getting across the meaning of a line in the way you say it. Over my ten years in The Loft I played many of the major roles. . . . I

learned, too, from James Stack as an elocution and drama teacher at the Cork School of Music. I always had great respect for Stacky. I was his pupil for seven years, including a year or two in his drama class as a teenager.'

Later, when Michael was

Dan Donovan, appearing in Half Way Up The Tree *in 1983.*
(© Everyman Palace)

appearing on cast lists of major productions in Cork, he was greatly influenced by Dan Donovan, once a pupil, then teacher, at Presentation College, the furnace-force in the college's Theatre Guild, who co-founded Everyman, which shapes theatre in the city to this very day.

> The one to whom I owe the most is Dan. What I learned from that man is immeasurable. In fact it is his style of directing that will always be there as long as I'm directing.
>
> At the same time I practise the extensive pre-rehearsal preparation and the precise approach I learned from James Stack. For example, I believe in the careful planning of movement. A movement can be used used to heighten the importance of a line, or to create a dramatic moment. I strive as much as I can to create the best visual effect possible for a scene. If a person came into a theatre and took a photo of the performance at any point, the composition of the picture created by the grouping of the characters on stage should look pleasing to the eye.
>
> To my amazement and disappointment, in some productions I have seen recently in the West End, that now appears to be less important. There is this striving for total naturalness, not alone in performance, but in the way actors stand on stage in relation to one another.

Michael has some fascinating insights into the wider world of the comedy actor. 'There is a great power in comedy. I remember Dublin comedian Jack Cruise, whose *Holiday*

Hayride shows were a huge hit with audiences. Jack was the master of the impeccably timed, crisply delivered punch-line.' But it was on a visit to the London Palladium in the early 1970s that Michael saw the incomparable Tommy Cooper live on stage.

> I'll always remember the opening of that show. It was a big dance number with sexy, high-kicking girls. The stage was decorated with a set of enormous playing cards in a semi-circle. The Joker suddenly revolved and there was Tommy in his dress suit and fez. He walked down the steps and stood at the microphone. He did not have to open his mouth – yet the audience burst into uncontrollable laughter. This, I thought, must be the ultimate in the power of comedy playing, where a comedian can grasp an audience in the palm of his hand without uttering a word.

Still on the subject of comedy, Michael harks back to the influences on his stage life and to Dan Donovan in particular:

> The contribution to comedy made by Dan is considerable. He directed a number of revues and played in several stage farces and comedies. Dan has a tremendous sense of humour himself and affection for all aspects of comedy, especially in its satirical and more sophisticated forms. His comprehensive knowledge of theatre-craft included an understanding of that essential component of comedy, timing, which he imparted to actors as required.

Chapter 2
Great Performers

Niall Toibín, Joe Lynch, Cecil Sheehan, Danny La Rue and Chris Curran

Michael and I reminisced about some of Cork's finest comedic talents who left their native city to pursue careers in Dublin and London. Their subsequent success on stage, radio, TV and film is a measure of their original genius for public performance, nurtured in their native city.

As Arts Editor at the *Irish Examiner*, I encountered the unique and multi-talented Mr Toibín. Niall is, in my view, the professionals' professional: authentic and razor-sharp in a myriad of diverse roles. He has done it all, and well; from his stunning Behan stage portrayals to the poignant Jim Nolan play, *Salvage Shop* (written for Red Kettle), as well as, of course, his many TV and feature film roles.

On one occasion, I was looking for someone to launch a book I had written. I hoped Niall would do it and he readily agreed, but previous commitments meant that he could not actually be there on the night. Although he never mentioned it, I was told that he had gone to enormous trouble to get back to Dublin, find a studio and get the launch speech down on video; it was riddled with witticisms and thoroughly enjoyed by all present.

He is one of Ireland's most versatile performers, straight or comic, and Michael suggests that Niall could be regarded as the link, even the stepping-stone, from the first joke-telling comedians to the modern, 'alternative' comedy. Michael says, 'He mainly extracts his humour from his observance of the

Niall Toibín in Cork to celebrate the 100ᵗʰ birthday party for the Everyman Palace Theatre.
(© Irish Examiner)

foibles and eccentricities of his fellow-countrymen, which he expertly weaves into his stories, complete with local accents, delivered with uncanny accuracy and a touch of devilment.'

Niall was a North Mon boy and it must be in the Northside air, because a succession of great artistes emerged from the Mon. There was, for instance, David McInerney, whom Niall remembers fondly as a great mimic.

Niall grew up in the 'radio age' and recalls sharing the laughter hours at home with his strict and serious father, as they listened to the Charlie Chester Show. Radio favourites at the time were Jimmy O'Dea on Radio 1 and live performer, Corkman Tadgh Foley, whom he says was 'gently naughty'.

Success in the Civil Service exams brought Niall to Dublin where he spent fourteen years with the Radio Éireann Repertory Players. Niall points out that he is not into deep analysis of the art of comedy but, subconsciously no doubt, through the broad repertoire of Irish drama he was developing that sense of the sound of the human voice and its accurate representation.

Niall has never seen himself and his art as being in any way comparable with the modern comedians. He does not particularly like the use of swear words in the 'new wave' comedy and says that the only time he used such words himself was when they were part of the characterisation. For Niall, his humour is all about accurate characterisation that the audience can identify with, no matter the county allegiance.

He loved being Father MacNally in the hit TV series, *Ballykissangel*. He feels that a set of excellent producers, particularly in the early days, helped establish the character. Even so, Niall had to make a stand when he felt there was danger that Father Mac could be portrayed as the 'Irish Paddy' priest: he got his way and Father Mac rang true to the character envisioned and fleshed out by Niall.

*

Another Cork 'exile' was Joe Lynch, again a most versatile performer, remembered still for his radio programme, *Living With Lynch*, as Dinny in RTÉ's TV series, *Glenroe*, and across the water for a series of outstanding TV performances, particularly in *Never Mind The Quality, Feel The Width*.

The late and great Joe Lynch
(© Private collection)

Michael recalls Joe's appearances in James Stack's *Holiday Revels*. 'I remember when, halfway through a number Joe popped up in the orchestra pit, took the baton from the conductor and drove the music on with wild abandon.'

On another occasion Cha and Miah were waiting off-set in a live TV show. They were nervously going over their lines when Joe began chatting to the two lads about his days growing up in Cork. 'No chance to explain to Joe that we were still rehearsing as he kept up his reminiscences without pause. I have no idea to this day how we got through our sketch when we arrived in front of the camera,' says Michael.

*

Cecil Sheehan was also a favourite son of Cork. Michael recalls Cecil as a very popular panto dame with a style of playing not far removed from that of the great Ignatius Comerford.

> I remember him in pantos in the old Opera House, Father O'Leary Hall, St Francis' Hall, AOH, and Father Mathew Hall. One of his catchphrases was, 'I'll tell the guards and you'll be remanded in custard!'
>
> Cecil had a shop in Douglas Street, but his heart was in theatre. His sister Stella was a most attractive actress and appeared several times with the Theatre Guild in Presentation College on the Western Road (Pres.), and in James Stack productions. Cecil knew that he had to go to Dublin eventually to develop his career in theatre and this he did admirably.

Cecil Sheehan: his heart was in theatre.
(© Irish Examiner)

*

Danny Carroll from Horgans Buildings has achieved international stardom as the dazzlingly costumed Danny La Rue and his most recent Cork appearance in 2005 was on the Everyman Palace Theatre stage where he was acclaimed once more by his adoring fans.

Our final Corkman, Chris Curran, was a product of The Loft, home of the Cork Shakesperean Company directed by the famous Fr O'Flynn, and James Stack's drama classes. As was the case with Niall, Joe and Cecil, Chris had all the qualities for stage success as well as being an accomplished pianist (his Jimmy Durante take of 'The Lost Chord' was a show-stopper), but he too had to 'emigrate' to Dublin to find success in TV, radio and on stage. He married another outstanding performer, Josephine Scanlon, who played principal boy in a number of Cork pantos in the old Opera House.

Chapter 3
Only Slagging

The Slag Revue

Comedy theatre had been an integral part of Michael Twomey's life on stage. In the early 1960s Donal O'Donovan told Michael that he was putting on a revue in the Group Theatre on South Main Street. It was to be a series of sketches written by Colum Fehily, and titled *Slag*.

At that time Michael's day job was in the office of the Irish National Insurance Company. His boss was Jim Lannin, son of Joe Lannin, a great Cork entertainer at the piano. Jim obviously understood the odd absence or visit to the office counter by Michael's theatrical friends. Michael was to make a very successful career in insurance but managed at the same time to enjoy his 'other life' on stage, and later on TV and film.

The Slag Revues took Cork by storm in the 1960s and the little Group Theatre in South Main Street would be jammed for weeks:

It was a wonderfully intimate theatre but facilities there were nil. I always remember the 'dressing rooms' right next to the stage, almost in the wings. James N. Healy had built a floor halfway up the wall, so you went up a ladder to where there was a sort of platform. That was a dressing room space. During a show there was great tearing up the ladder, changing costume and tearing down again for your cue.

Somehow it worked, and it was from my time in the *Slag* shows that I learned an awful lot about comedy and how a show of that type was designed to work with such effect. They were so popular that we had to do midnight matinees. A show finished at half past ten and we'd go on again at 11.30. They'd run to packed houses for three weeks.

There can be a fine line between success and failure in show business. Michael is convinced, as are others, that the shows worked so well because of the writing of Colum Fehily:

Colum Fehily was the creative genius behind the Slag shows.
(© Fehily family)

Colum had the ability in writing satire to cut to the very core of the matter being dealt with. He was a political animal so he brought to his work a deep knowledge.

Donal O'Donovan, producer, had a remarkable imagination. There was the sketch called 'The Senators' where we were supposed to be a jazz band. We were all dressed in Roman togas. We all had instruments but mimed to a jazz record. The performance was so spot-on that the audience could not be certain if in fact the instruments were being played, which, for some of the tone-deaf cast, was mission impossible.

Every sacred cow was tackled by Colum. He had an incredible insight into his subjects. Even theatre people did not escape his barbs and the baloney attached to elite theatre also came under his scalpel.

One of his most famous sketches concerned an interview for a job on the South Mall. One applicant had all the degrees and qualifications necessary. The second had failed every exam he had ever attempted. His only claim to fame was that he played rugger and there was a strong possibility that he would play for Ireland.

The unfortunate first interviewee was chess champion of Ireland and had passed all his exams with top class honours. He was a multi-linguist, but there was no way he was getting the job, once it was learned that the other 'failed' student might soon don the green rugby jersey.

Charlie Hennessy played the luckless chess player; Michael Twomey was the oval ball type and Donal O'Donovan, the office manager. The whole sketch was another example of art imitating life in a class-conscious age when jobs were few and opportunity could come down to skill on the field of play.

Michael's playing of that role of the future rugby star has some irony about it, remembering that his mother had put her foot down when he showed some promise at the game in 'Pres'.

The second most memorable sketch concerned the training of a sports reporter being tutored by an experienced hack. Having ensured that the debutant scribe reaches for every possible sporting cliché in recalling the scoring of a goal in a match, the older man says he must end the lesson as he has to review a play in the Opera House; no doubt with suitable hyperbole and mixing of a few metaphors in the process.

But before heading off he rings through to the Opera House and asks the manager what the show was like, suggesting that the audience might indeed be rolling in the aisles. Fortunately he is corrected. 'Oh it's a tragedy. I'm glad you mentioned that . . . anyway, thanks for that and I suppose I can say that James N. Healy was his own inimitable self.' Call ends, review done and junior reporter is suitably impressed.

Then there was the sketch about the Film Festival. An old toff is in a dress suit, silk scarf draped around neck, talking to a TV reporter about who was, and who was not, at a lavish reception at the Festival Club. After much name-dropping, the reporter asks the toff what were the films like. 'Oh! – Are there films, too,?' comes the incredulous reply.

Nothing was deemed sacred in those *Slag* shows and the proof that Cork audiences loved them is that they are still spoken of with deep affection. Michael feels that this period taught him so much about good comedy and the fine art of timing. Also, he learned just how important it was to 'point' a line, to give it the right emphasis.

He remembers Colum's brilliant sketch of two fellows in a pub (played by Michael and Charlie Hennessy), which was a little like something from Beckett or Pinter. There was a series of silences punctuated by apparently unconnected references such as 'Cuba . . . a dog . . . the missus.' Michael knows now that this sketch was in fact the stylistic seed from which the famous Cha and Miah sketches (between Frank Duggan and Michael) were to blossom.

'Donal O'Donovan developed a show structure for the *Slags* which was ahead of its time in Irish theatre,' recalls Michael. 'Tabs (curtains) were used, which meant that when one sketch was finished the set could be changed at the same time as another item was being performed in front of the tabs. Siobhán O'Brien might be doing a solo Edith Piaf song while the rest of the cast were changing for the next scene, featuring a new set, different props.'

Interestingly, although we now have modern stand-up comics, unabashed about affronting people's sensibilities with their brazen 'in your face' style, the *Slag* shows of those times might attract some criticism in this age of political correctness. And no doubt the much-publicised national tribunals in Dublin Castle would have been fertile ground for the late and great Colum Fehily.

When the new Opera House was opened by President Eamon de Valera on 31 October 1965, the historic stage show that evening featured a special satirical sketch with Michael Twomey, Cathal Stenson (Charlie Hennessy), Jos Cahill, Donal O'Donovan and Charlie Ginnane. Written specially by Colum Fehily, it had the 'Slaggers' looking back to the old Opera House days.

Chapter 4
The Keane Edge

John B. Keane, *Summer Revels* and Pantomime in Cork

Michael Twomey is, in a sense, a 'victim' of his own versatility. His career, particularly in theatre and to a lesser extent on film and TV, covered such a broad portfolio of work that it is nigh impossible to measure his achievement. Michael has earned the respect of his full-time professional peers in the theatre world.

In the course of more than sixty years, Michael has been an actor in some of the most talked-about plays in Irish professional theatre, a director of a succession of classic dramas, President of the Association of Drama Adjudicators and a member of the board of the Everyman Palace Theatre, one of the most successful and prolific promoting houses of good theatre in the country.

John B. Keane and Cork theatre proved a potent combination from Keane's very first play, *Sive*, and its professional première in 1959 in the Father Mathew Hall.

Michael says, 'On a personal level I had a special affinity with John B.'s plays, first as an actor and then as a director. I directed a version of *Sive* for the Opera House that won several awards from the drama critics. I directed *Sharon's Grave, Many Young Men Of Twenty, The Field* and *Matchmake Me Do* for the Everyman Palace.'

I asked Michael how important comedy was in the many John B. Keane plays in which he had acted or directed. 'John B. was writing about the type of characters he knew well. It was a rural humour. He was able to inject a humorous phrase into a serious situation with great effect.'

In *The Man From Clare* – about the decline of a gaelic footballer – Pakie and Petey were there to lighten a situation. Pakie, out of nowhere, says: 'I knew wan once and her hair was blue.' The line had absolutely nothing to do with the scene but it had an uproarious effect on the audiences.

In rehearsal John B. Keane's The Man From Clare *with (l. to r.) Murt Kelleher, Michael Twomey, Seán Healy, Charlie Ginnane and Ber Power*
(© DonaL Sheehan)

Michael has always tried to avoid that which he decides is vulgar or distasteful on stage. He is conscious that things have changed incredibly since those days when a swear word in a script would be a matter of long discussion.

> When we got the script of *Many Young Men of Twenty* from John B. in 1961, there was a scene where Danger Mullally is standing on a chair singing a song. At the end he says: 'Get me down off the shaggin' chair.' James N. Healy, Dan Donovan and myself seriously considered whether we could leave in that word 'shaggin''. Should we change it to 'bloody' or 'damn'? We agonised as to whether it was too much for sensitive ears. We left it in to see how it would go on the first night. It brought the house down. It was a lesson.

Curtain call for Sive *at the Olympia*
(© Private Collection)

Michael's association with John B. has spanned a crowded career ever since *Sive* shook the cosy world of Irish theatre and had everybody talking about the man from Listowel. It may not be everyone's favourite Keane play (*Sharon's Grave* with Maura Hassett as Trassie and *The Year Of The Hiker* remain my own personal top two), but a stand-out production for many was a version of *Many Young Men Of Twenty* in 2006 at the Everyman Palace, directed by Michael. A strong cast included: Hugh Moynihan, Tony Callanan, Shane Casey, Kevin O'Meara, Loraine Manley, Conor Dwane, Ian McGuirk, Rebecca Allman, Valery O'Leary, Ronnie O'Shaughnessy, Tony Hegarty, Deirdre O'Riordan, and Michael Murphy.

There was a freshness to the production and I look forward to the years when new companies will revisit John B.'s work and capture the excitement first engendered when *Sive* was performed by the Listowel Players and then brought to a wider audience by Dan Donovan, James N. Healy and Frank Sanquest. Equally worthy of mention was Michael's direction of *Matchmake Me Do*, with Kevin Sheehan, Tony Hegarty, Paddy Comerford, Ronnie O'Shaughnessy, Kevin O'Meara, Jo Cronin and Mary Foley at the Everyman Palace in 2002.

*

When Michael looks back on a career that has included so many different aspects of public performance (from pantomime to high drama, revue to major musicals) and continues apace, he considers that he has been very lucky in the people with whom he has worked, both on and off stage.

My first venture into panto in the early 1960s was with the late Bill Mahony and Noreen Godsil – a company we called GMT Productions at St Francis Hall in Sheares Street. It was *Cinderella*, produced by Bill, who also played Buttons, and starred Cecil Sheehan and Josephine Scanlon.

Bill became quite ill just before Christmas and I spent Christmas Day at his bedside learning the part of Buttons, which I played at the matinee and night shows on St Stephen's Day until Bill was well enough to take over.

At the time, in the late '50s and '60s there could be seven pantos in Cork. The venues included: Opera House, Father Mathew Hall (Fr Mathew Street), Father O'Leary Hall (Bandon Road), AOH Hall (Morrison's Island), St Francis Hall (Sheares Street), Cork Catholic Young Men's Society (CCYMS) Little Theatre (Castle Street), and Gurraneabraher Hall. There could have been two or more versions of the same panto but they all did the business.

He also recalls those who made shows happen by their contribution in the important months before opening performance. There was Peggy McTeggart and her Irish dancers who did so many great numbers in the later productions of *Summer Revels* and the pantos. Peggy used to come up with remarkable scenes, such as her take on *Riverdance*. There was also Donna Daly and her dancers. Donna was a co-producer of the smash hit, *Singing in the Rain* from Golden Boy Productions, in which Michael appeared: although not in the première run at the Palace, he was with the show in Dublin for six weeks at the Olympia and then back in Cork for the second run at the Palace. I also had the privilege to work with the late

David Gordon, choreographer and director, who gave so much of his talent to musical theatre and ballet in Cork.

> A very happy memory of my stage life was when it had been decided what panto we'd be doing in the Opera House. In October or early November, I'd visit Eileen Cavanagh in her flat over Woodford Bourne's in Patrick Street.
>
> Invariably, the weather was cold and Eileen always had a roaring fire going. There'd always be tea and cakes in a big spread on the table. First question was: 'What are we doing this year?' I'd say *Aladdin* or some other panto. She'd say: 'I have just the right idea for that now.' She'd come up with a 'spesh'; a scene that was done by her dance group which may not have any connection to the show itself but was the troupe's showcase.

Eileen Nolan's troupe, the Montforts, was also integral to these annual shows, both *Summer Revels* and pantos.

> They were a very hard working group who rehearsed diligently and they had their own choreographers and resident musical director in Ronnie O'Shaughnessy. Ronnie was a pianist, conductor and musical director for the entire show. She was an advisor and voice trainer for the Montforts. She never did appear on stage in *Summer Revels*, or in the pantos, although she is a very good comedy actor in her own right as she showed in her hilarious role in *Matchmake Me Do*. In her early days, Ronnie and her sister Imelda were part

of the Eileen Cavanagh troupe in panto in the old Opera House.

The contribution of the Montforts to those shows could not be measured. People still remind me about their big numbers such as 'The Scottish Scene' or 'New York, New York'. They were very important in *Summer Revels* as they were the very attractive 'book-enders'. They'd open the show, do the final number before the interval, open the second half and would be involved again in the grand finale.

As a director I love to be surrounded by people that I work with regularly. It creates a family atmosphere but it also makes things much easier for me as they know in advance what I want, sometimes even before I ask for it. It also helped when I knew whom I was writing for in a particular script.

Mention of scripts reminds me to record the invaluable contribution made by Frank Duggan to the writing of sketches, particularly the renowned Shakesperean sketches which we wrote in iambic pentameter with rhyming couplets.

I could not emphasise enough the input of Pat Murray as a designer in *Revels* and pantos. I'd meet Pat in his house on the Rochestown Road a couple of months beforehand. We'd talk about the various sketches and big musical numbers. Pat's genius lay in not only coming up with magnificent sets, but he would do it in such a way that there was an easy transition from a sketch into a big musical item. When he was designing a set he always had in mind how would we go from say, an airport scene, straight into a Scottish number by the Montforts. Quite often he'd design the costumes as well to enhance the overall look of a show. His input was always immense.

I was lucky in that I worked with great musicians and singers. There was the late Noel Frost, one of the finest accordionists of his time, in the early *Revels*. Another brilliant musician is Donal Ring Jnr of céilí fame, and Aideen Crowley Dynan is always a popular turn on the xylophone.

Michael is married to Marie Twomey, a star in her own right, having first appeared in a string of musicals performed at the St

Aloysius School and graduating to the Opera House stage in a succession of major productions down the years. She appeared in over half of the *Summer Revels* shows in which her duets with Dave McInerney were a popular feature.

Michael reminisces, 'There were so many other singers that I have enjoyed working with over the years. They include Hugh Moynihan, Deirdre White, Shirley McCarthy, Christy Morris, Lorraine Manley, Linda Kenny and so many others. All were capable of stepping

A Summer Revels star Marie Twomey
(© Joe McCarthy)

into an acting role in the very next sketch such was their versatility.'

*

And then, of course, there were those unforgettable panto dames. Michael considers that Billa O'Connell's dame was unique:

> It is very rarely that you will find a dame as masculine, or indeed, as macho . . . [as Billa], dressed up as a woman and deliberately making no effort to conceal his masculinity. This is where he scores comedy-wise. The comedy is in his characterisation. Billa is the very antithesis to Danny La Rue and his portrayal of feminity. And yet Billa, under his wife's [Nell Cotter] sure guidance, was very particular about his costume, down to his shoes. He always carried a handbag on stage. He'd hang it on the stand which held the microphone. It was always part of his character. Billa took particular care of his wigs. I remember hairdresser Pat O'Donovan coming into the Opera House to look after those wigs.
>
> The fun in Billa was that everybody knew it was Billa, a man pretending to be a woman. He made brilliant use of certain catchphrases. Having told a joke, he'd fix his gaze on someone in the audience and shout, 'Explain that to her.' There was the standard claim that he had forgotten his lines and the audience would break up with laughter. It all came across as spontaneous but it was carefully studied and rehearsed. That was the genius of Billa.

Paddy Comerford in drag had much the same approach as Billa. In his act he'd lean slightly more towards femininity, but he was a very brazen female. Both were brilliant as the Ugly Sisters in *Cinderella* and as lady friends in the various sketches.

Billa O' Connell, Tony Hegarty and Paddy Comerford onstage in Cinderella *at the Opera House 1986/7*
(© private collection)

Tony Hegarty is another one of the outstanding dames, following on the same lines as Billa and Paddy, but more a mix of the two. Again we have a macho man who is funny because he's pretending to be a woman.

Postcard from the edge – Tony is all dressed up
complete with accessory handbag
(© private collection)

Interestingly, all of us in *Summer Revels* did a bit
of drag. There was the sketch the Tulips of Cork, a
thinly disguised skit on the *Rose of Tralee* contest. The
ban gardaí sketch was equally 'arresting' as were the
appearances of the 'Mothers of Seven' at their coffee
mornings. The audiences loved seeing the entire male
cast dressed as women.

Very much in the traditional role of the panto
dame is Jim Mulcahy. Having seen him in a number
of pantos in the Everyman in recent years, he really is
in the mould of the Cork panto dame.

Donie Gleeson's alter ego, Shirley Chassis, is a real crowd-pleaser. Apart from his stage appearances in various comedy and variety shows, Donie is a most accomplished cabaret performer. Once again, it is indigenous humour and he has the necessary ability to establish a rapport with his audience.

Audiences may not realise fully how much we have been blessed with the success of great panto dames, going right back to the great Ignatius Comerford. He was on the same level as Jimmy O'Dea and, in my memory, would be one of the most loved and original of all Cork dames.

Michael Twomey never did play the dame, but he was a stand-in for an Ugly Sister in *Cinderella*. 'I enjoyed it. I was also a ban garda and one of "Tulips" of Cork!'

Chapter 5
Take a Bow

Recalling People and Productions

Michael Twomey is delighted to pay tribute to the many multi-talented people who have graced Cork stages down the years – those people who worked tirelessly to ensure that each night's performance was the best possible. 'Take Dick Healy,' he says, 'who is usually thought of as an outstanding stage manager – but he was an invaluable straight man in the comedy sketches. He was always the barman with Cha and Miah. We always gave him at least one gag to interject which brought the house down. He was the MC in the 'Rose of Tralee' skit; he was the male garda sergeant receiving the reports from the unlikely ban garda line-up; he was one of the grumpy old men in the hospital sketches and the obstreperous maid in 'Mothers of Seven'. He would combine his major role as stage manager with all these characterisations.

Over the years guest performers took leading roles in Cork pantos, particularly at the Opera House. Colin Baker, who was the treacherous Paul Meroney in the hit TV series *The Brothers*, came to Cork to be Dick Whittington on the only occasion that the panto was performed in the Opera House. Colin went on to achieve further fame as TV's Doctor Who.

Opera House manager Dick Hill decided that Vicki Michelle – Sally O'Brien to TV viewers – should get in the panto act. Later Vicki was to be Rene's secret lover in *'Allo, 'Allo*. Other guests were comedian Noel V. Ginnity and Joe Conlon who played Buttons in a production of *Cinderella*. Tony Kenny played a number of pantos in Cork and his wife Joan joined him in a production of *Aladdin*. Actor Martin Dempsey was an excellent giant in *Jack and the Beanstalk*. Sandy Jones, Fran Dempsey and Nicola Kerr all took to panto. Not their usual style, but actors Gerry McLoughlin, Michael McAuliffe and singer Jimmy Crowley also joined in the festive frolics. Michael's special panto memories include the remarkable revolving set designed by the late Pat Murray for a staging of *Goldilocks and the Three Bears*, and the scary performances by Pat Talbot as 'Count Dragemoff' and 'The Giant'.

My own first experience of working with Michael came in the millennium year when he agreed to direct a show I had written, *Up the Rebels*. In the city itself we knew we had a ready-made audience, because we knew the fans would like what we did; but we were not at all sure how a potted history of the GAA in Cork, performed on stage with music and a large helping of humour, would fare with a wider audience. The original concept was a somewhat unwieldy affair and it was the genius of Michael that ensured it was the success it turned out to be.

The rehearsal phase holds fond memories for us all. Courtesy of the *Examiner*, we rehearsed in the newspaper's training room, with its bank of screens that could be carefully moved aside each evening and then put back in place a few hours later. That room in its way represented the huge advances being made at a technological level and there we were – director, writer, actors – attempting to capture theatrically the history of the GAA all the way back to its founding more than 116 years before.

Up The Rebels!: *Michael Twomey, Declan Hassett, Linda Kenny and Tony Hegarty*
(© private collection)

Theatre is a close-knit community, which can be viewed from a distance as a cosy, almost elitist coterie, but my experience has been the opposite. I have found that, individually and collectively, these people are a generous, talented group who love nothing more than an audience and are seldom more than a few lines away from a stage. I have felt for some time now that the wider community, those in authority and in commerce, do not always appreciate the contribution the stage arts make to a modern society where the fiscal 'bottom line' is the narrow measure of importance and success.

In Ireland there is a sort of lip-service paid to the arts, but I believe modern society neglects them at its peril. All those who are the subject of this book, or are mentioned in passing, have enriched our lives. The appreciation of that fact should be reflected in an even greater support of theatre, which transports us out of the mundane, the humdrum of our everyday existence.

Even at the most frenetic of rehearsals, there is a pervasive fun and banter evident. Invariably those same people would have come from day jobs, grabbed a cup of tea and headed out again for rehearsals. For the writer the rehearsal period is a special time, as the script is now in the hands of the director and the lines take a life of their own as the actors move through each scene. Production was by Tony Hegarty, much loved comedian; for this particular play, however, it was his love and knowledge of GAA matters that made the difference.

Michael Twomey's field passion is Manchester United and he is not really a regular patron of Croke Park and Páirc Uí Chaoimh, though one of his stage personas, Miah, has been known to pontificate on the fine art of 'hurley', much to the admiration of his 'buttie', Cha.

The cast list for *Rebels* led by Kevin Sheehan was particularly strong. Michael had this to say about Kevin: 'He was one of the finest actors, straight and comedy, ever to appear on a Cork stage. His Polonius in *Hamlet* was the best I have seen, yet he could go into a Keane play and capture a comedy character perfectly.' For *Up the Rebels* he was to become Eudie Coughlan, the legendary Blackrock man who drove Cork to victory after that incredible three-match All-Ireland final in 1931. Kevin's

performance as Eudie has taken on a legendary status of its own. It was as if the young fisherman, who had worked all his life with the Harbour Board, had come back to remind us that 1931 would be remembered long after other years were forgotten. Re-creating legend is indeed a tricky business but Kevin Sheehan as Eudie was truly memorable. Kevin now lives in Dublin and the loss of that great character actor to Cork theatre is immeasurable.

From a production point of view *Up the Rebels* presented Michael Twomey with several, mainly technical, challenges, as we attempted to marry traditional stage presentation with what we considered to be the fine art of back-projection. Crucial were the video shots of Christy Ring, brilliantly filmed years before by Louis Marcus. There was, too, the poignant recall of Jack Lynch's funeral passing through his beloved Cork.

And then there were wonderful comic interludes from Cha and Miah and Tony Hegarty as Bould Thady Quill. Jokes do not usually travel well from page to stage, but Cha demonstrated the famous Cork wit when he told Miah, in the Christy Ring scene, that a famous Tipperary goalkeeper was once seen running on to the old Athletic Grounds with two hurleys under his arm. When his pal asked what was the need for *two* hurleys, Cha's reply was swift: 'One is for pucking the ball out and the other for letting it in.' Pat Murray designed our set and Ronnie O'Shaughnessy was an ideal Musical Director.

Watching Michael in those frenetic weeks prior to opening confirmed for me that things work well as long as the homework is done. The contribution made by Cork County Board to the millennium year may not have been properly appreciated at the time, but the then Vice Chairman, Jim

Forbes, Secretary Frank Murphy and Chairman Jim Cronin were all particularly supportive. Michael Twomey recalls:

> *Rebels* was one of the most challenging productions in my time in theatre. I felt, initially, that I was the wrong director for this. It was a mix of comedy, narration, music, pageantry. I was very lucky to have Tony Hegarty as producer and a cast which included Kevin Sheehan, Frank Duggan, Conor Dwane, Linda Kenny and, second time around, Lorraine Manley. There was the complex use of technology, but we put it together; and boy, did it work. Frank and myself loved doing the Cha and Miah/Christy Ring scene in that show.

I asked Michael what his favourite roles had been and the plays that, as a director, had given him the most satisfaction.

> Over the years it would be Professor Higgins in the Opera House production of *My Fair Lady* with Brid Hartnett as Eliza and Jim Queally as Pickering. I loved playing the title role in *Quartermain's Terms* directed by that stalwarth of Cork theatre John O'Shea; then there was Jack in *Home* directed by June McCarthy, Father in *I Never Sang for my Father* directed by Michael McCarthy and Juror No. 9 in *Twelve Angry Men* so well directed by Marion Wyatt, whose work as a drama teacher and director has introduced much new talent to Cork theatre; and of course, my first *Hamlet* directed by Eileen Curran and Fr O'Flynn which won a number of awards at

the Killarney Drama Festival. In retrospect I feel some regret that years later I foolishly attempted to direct *and* play *Hamlet* at the Opera House for Theatre of the South. I learned then that if you try to direct and play a leading role one or the other will suffer. I was fortunate in this production to have Dan Donovan playing King Claudius and my wife Marie playing my mother Queen Gertrude.

The productions that gave me great satisfaction as a director include *Death of a Salesman* and *All My Sons* – both with Dan Donovan and Lorna Daly; *An Ideal Husband, The Country Girl*, and *An Inspector Calls* all featuring London actor David Lumsden; but my favourite perhaps are *The Constant Wife* with one of the best sets ever designed by Pat Murray, and for sheer fun and enjoyment John B. Keane's *Matchmake Me Do* – all for the Everyman Theatre Company.

As I've said I owe an immense debt of gratitude to Dan Donovan from whom I learned so much and to James N. Healy who was another great teacher particularly of the business aspects of a production.

The Insurevues, as the name suggests, were a series of shows put on at the Group Theatre and directed by Michael for the Insurance Institute. Not as bitingly satirical as the *Slag* shows, they were very popular with insurance colleagues. Frank Duggan was accompanist. Proceeds went to the Institute's charities and the news of the show's success spread; so much so that Niall O'Flynn, from the *Tops of the Town*, asked Michael to do something similar for the new Cork competition that was going to be staged at the School of Music Auditorium. The Insurance and Beamish & Crawford theatre groups came top out of fourteen groups in total: it is worth adding that the leading star in the Beamish show was a certain Billa O'Connell. The final of the competition was held in the Palace Theatre and was won by the *Insurevue*.

It happened that Theatre of the South was planning its summer season at the Opera House and James N. felt that a revue-type show could make a valuable contribution to the usual summer season programme at the Opera House. Michael was asked to expand on the show that he had staged for the Tops competition and invited Billa as the guest artiste. Thus the first *Summer Revels* went on in 1971, with the hope that it might run for a week or two. In the end, it ran for seven weeks – and then for twenty-one years after that.

One of the sketches called for someone to play a crotchety old man. At the time there was another play in rehearsal in the theatre. Someone suggested that one of the cast from that other play, Paddy Comerford, might fit the bill. Michael had an Uncle Peter, so Paddy adopted the name and evolved a Chaplinesque personality in vest, braces, old brown pants and jacket, complete with scarf and bowler hat.

Now the *Revels* cast boasted Billa, Paddy and Cha (Frank Duggan) and Miah (Michael Twomey) – what a comedic line-up. It got better – eventually former *Swans* show comedy duo, Pat Sullivan and Noel Barrett, also joined the cast. The show had a sure-fire formula with a big opening, middle and closure from the Montforts, directed by Eileen Nolan. The late Pat Murray came up with magnificent sets. His art came from his wonderful imagination. He used pillars of light and had *Summer Revels* in lit scroll (enlarged lettering lit up by stage spotlights usually suspended against a backdrop), different for each year.

So it came about that this so-called 'filler' show was enjoyed by Cork audiences for over two decades, with Dick Healy as stage-manager and his wife, Sheila, in charge of costuming.

Revels, butties and bar stools – Frank Duggan, Dick Healy and Michael Twomey discussing world affairs
(© Private Collection)

*

Chapter 6
Slates on Churches

Cha and Miah, Paddy Joe and Cork Pantomime

Cha and Miah became huge attractions through their appearances on Frank Hall's TV show, *Hall's Pictorial Weekly*; they were sought all over the country and they put an awful lot of slates on churches as the stars of fund-raiser shows.

Then, of course, there was that other Michael Twomey institution: Paddy Joe Canavaun from Tooreendohenybeg, self-appointed expert on all matters rural. Michael recalls, 'We filmed those sketches on a friend's farm in the Whitecross area. Frank played the unfortunate reporter sent down by Montrose to interview the great man. Paddy had a great sense of community because he tried to establish a ballet company in Tooreendohenybeg. In fact he demonstrated some fancy steps 'his-self'. The late Joe Kerrigan was a great provider of props for these sketches.'

In the early 1970s Dublin theatre impresario and film producer Noel Pearson asked Cha and Miah if they would guest in a panto he was staging at the Opera House in Cork. Michael felt from the beginning that it was a mistake: 'Cha and Miah were not knock-about comedians. We were too laid-back for panto. It was a struggle each night to get a script across as the kids were yelling, "look out, he's behind ya". But that was not to say that we did not enjoy the experience. We ended up having great fun.'

Noel then asked Michael if he would direct the next panto. Michael says, 'That began an association with panto in the Opera House which spanned thirty years. Eventually I scripted as well as directed. The last panto I did at the Opera House was the Christmas of 1999 which ran into the new millennium.' For those panto years at the big theatre, Michael relied on stalwarts of the *Summer Revels* team, featuring Billa O'Connell as the dame, with Paddy Comerford, The Montforts, and later Barrett and Sullivan.

In 1990 the Opera House decided that it would stage a different, modern-style panto, so the Everyman Palace approached Michael to direct their first Christmas panto at the MacCurtain Street venue.

In 1992 the Opera House reverted to the traditional panto and Michael and his team crossed the River Lee again; the Cork Academy of Dramatic Arts (CADA), under the direction of Catherine Mahon Buckley, took over at the Everyman Palace.

Michael has strong views on the subject of panto production: 'Panto is essentially for children, with the fairy tale stories of *Cinderella, Babes in the Wood, Jack and the Beanstalk, Red Riding Hood*, et cetera, and the secret was to stage these in such a way that would appeal especially to young audiences. Furthermore they should remain true to the original stories as far as possible, but delivered with great humour and plenty of music. Billa agreed with this approach and his huge success in panto was mainly due to his great rapport with children.'

The script, too, had to have a topical element that appealed not only to the children but also to the accompanying adults. The panto was vital to the commercial health of a theatre venue as it provided an enormous cash flow to kick-start the year's programme. Michael recalls being in the Opera House backstage on many a Christmas Eve, preparing for the then traditional opening of the panto on St Stephen's Day.

> If you were involved you could forget Christmas as a holiday time, because even on Christmas Day itself you were still worrying about this and that. Then you headed for the theatre first thing on Stephen's morning. It was a pressure on family life for everybody involved. All of us had to have very understanding wives, husbands, girlfriends, boyfriends and, indeed, children. You were really not able to concentrate on a family Christmas as the panto was hanging over you.
>
> That pressure eased in later years when pantos began opening before Christmas in the second week of December. You did start rehearsals earlier than before, but with the early opening there was not as much emphasis, from a production point of view, on the matinee and evening shows on St Stephen's Day.

It should not be forgotten that all the members of a production, with the exception of the resident backstage people, had day jobs. Once Christmas week was over, there was the added burden of the early morning start at the office or factory. Then, in the evening, there was just enough time for a quick bite to eat and off to the theatre for that night's show and no return home in sight until midnight. It took a particular discipline for those who were leading double lives, as it were, between the daily routine and the more exciting, but also more energetic, evenings on stage.

The Opera House stage crew were a remarkable bunch of men, as Michael remembers well:

> Paddy O'Leary did the lighting in the Opera House. Paddy was so good he'd anticipate your needs. Tommy Burke was incredible in his backstage production role. If you wanted a sedan chair for the arrival of the blundering baron in the panto, Tommy would make it and make it well. Even the coach for Cinderella would be his work. One year he even looked after the little ponies which pulled the coach each evening. Tommy saw to their needs in a makeshift stable in the old *Examiner* garage on Half Moon Street, and ensured that the little animals had their walk every day, even though they were quartered in the centre of the city. All that was beyond the call of duty but part of his interest and anxiety that everything should be right for the show itself.
>
> Then there was Christy Donovan, or, as he was affectionately known to all theatre people, Christy 'Props'. No matter what you wanted, be it an umbrella, a suitcase, a lamp, Christy produced it from somewhere.
>
> Also an invaluable member of the backstage crew in later years was Tom Cuthbert, who in fact had performed himself in the *Up Cork!* shows and pantos.

Pantomime Babes in The Wood *at Fr O' Leary Hall, December 1961 with Tom Cuthbert as the Dame.*
(© Irish Examiner)

You always received a great welcome from Bill Cunningham at the stage door – a nice, quiet, decent gentleman – and then there was Nora Malone looking after everyone at the bar in the Green Room. It was like one big family. All the cast and backstage staff during the run of the panto looked after each other.

There was the banter and inevitable ball-hopping too. I have often wondered what makes Cork humour so effective. Michael Twomey believes that the Cork humour works because of the accent, the idiom, the unique turn of phrase: 'It is uniquely attractive to audiences outside of Cork.'

Summer Revels, too, had its largely unsung heroes. The *Revels* season gave the Opera House valuable cash flow, and at each performance there was a raffle to gather funds for the theatre's refurbishment. This was organised by Jim O'Brien, Eileen Nolan's father, who was himself a seasoned performer, well known for his appearances as The Baron in pantos at the Father Mathew Hall. He also wrote a number of pantos; indeed, some of the Opera House pantos in the 1970s and 1980s were based on storylines by Jim.

Chapter 7
Cha and Miah

Given all that has been achieved by Michael Twomey, it comes almost as a contradiction that he will be best remembered for his portrayal on TV and stage as Miah of Cha and Miah fame, surely the best known and most loved Corkmen on the whole of the island of Ireland.

In life, being there in the right place at the right time is quite often the key to success. The *Slag* shows had already paraded before an adoring theatre public the first characters in the Cha and Miah mould – creations of the fertile brains of Messrs Colum Fehily and Donal O'Donovan, fleshed out by Charlie Hennessy and Michael Twomey. Actually that is not strictly correct, as Charlie Hennessy was then Cathal Stenson. The legal profession would not be too happy having its most promising young solicitor doubling as a 'Slagger' by night. So 'Cathal' and Michael were the forerunners of Cha and Miah.

Enter stage right Frank Duggan, some-time accompanist on *Slag* shows and colleague, with Michael, of the Insurance Institute. It was all to happen one afternoon on the South Mall,

Cork's professional quarter – once a canal where merchant princes 'parked' the Cork equivalent of a gondola beneath arched limestone berths before making their way up stone steps to offices on the floors above.

'Tis Like Dis Like: Miah (Michael Twomey) puts things on the long finger for buttie Cha (Frank Duggan)
(© Joe McCarthy)

At the time Frank Hall was doing an RTÉ 1 show called *Newsbeat*. Another much-loved Corkman Bill O'Herlihy was his out-and-about reporter. In 1969 he happened to be doing a vox pop on the South Mall. The subject was the danger of smoking to one's health. As it happened, Frank Duggan met Bill on the street. Bill and Frank – great friends, best men at each other's weddings – got chatting. Frank suggested that there could be a bit of fun in setting up an imaginary interview with a Cork character. He thought that Michael Twomey might be agreeable to play the character.

Michael was about to leave the office when Frank and Bill

approached him with the idea for a sketch. There and then Michael and Frank wrote the script on a piece of paper. Michael borrowed a coat and cap from the porter who had his flat on the top floor of the office block, and the mock interview was filmed.

The sketch went out on RTÉ and there was a terrific reaction, not just to the content, but also to the Cork accent of this strange man in coat and cap who would become Ireland's own Miah. Michael recalls:

> It was as if the nation realised for the first time that there was a Cork accent. It had such comic potential. After Frank Hall saw the first sketch on the Mall, he wanted more of the same, but rather than having me talking to myself in a monologue, it was fortunately decided that I would be joined by Frank, thus the real Cha was born. It was as simple as that. Frank brought his own natural acting to bear in creating and developing the character of Cha, making him a complete contrast to Miah.

Good scripting was a vital element of the Cha and Miah sketches. The two characters were loved nationwide and Frank Hall was aware of this, right from the early scenes. He recognised their importance in the context of the programme screened at peak teatime after the main news. Michael says, 'The names Cha and Miah were used originally by Donal O'Donovan and myself in a sketch that we did for Donacha O Dulaing who was hosting a series of radio concerts from the old Cork School of Music Auditorium.'

Cha and Miah became household names, thanks to the

popularity of Frank Hall's *Newsbeat* and, later, his *Pictorial Weekly*. Cork-based cameraman Joe McCarthy and Paul O'Flynn on sound ensured that Ireland stood up and took notice of the men from the banks of the Lee.

Cha and Miah are what you might call 'slow comedy' characters. They're laid-back – the very opposite to knockabout. Often there are more pregnant pauses than you would find in Pinter. Pauses accompanied by looks and facial expressions as 'slow minds sought to grasp meanings'. You had a touch of the Samuel Becketts too. The pauses and the timing were refined by audience reaction in each performance. You could say that Cha and Miah were a static, visual comedy. Very like Laurel and Hardy when they were not in knockabout mode. But, more accurately, Cha and Miah were a sort of Peter Cooke and Dudley Moore. I have always maintained that when accents are used in performance it is important for the actor to be conscious of articulation, so that the accent does not drown the words. I believe Cha and Miah's nation-wide popularity was due in no small measure to the fact that our words could be clearly understood by viewers everywhere.

In the early '80s I toured England with the late renowned tenor Frank Patterson as the compère of his concert. We played in six English cities, including a St Patrick's Night concert in the Royal Albert Hall in London before an audience of five thousand. I told exactly the same comedy stories as I would at any concert in Ireland using various accents – city and rural. I'm delighted to say they received a tremendous response everywhere, mainly because the audiences could understand without difficulty what I was saying.

Chapter 8
Radio Days

Frank Duggan

It was radio, not stage or TV, which first honed the visually brilliant, comedic skills of Frank Duggan as Cha.

Frank was a good listener. Entertainment in the homes of Ireland in the 1950s, prior to the invasion of Radio Telefís Éireann in the early 1960s, was radio-based, with the record-player assuming an increasingly unimportant role in the corner, or even banished to the end of the hall.

In the Duggan household, Sunday evenings and weekdays were dominated by the 'must-hear' shows of the time, featuring Tommy Handley, Eric Barker and Arthur Askey, whose catch-phrase was 'I thank you'. Richard Murdoch was the star of *Much Binding in the Marsh*, and later there was *Beyond Our Ken* and *Round the Horne* with Kenneth Horne. Then on Sunday evenings you had *Variety Bandbox* with top of the bill stars such as Frankie Howerd.

'I loved comedy on radio. I suppose, subconsciously, I was

honing whatever modicum of comedy skill I had acquired over the years,' admits Frank with genuine humility, in spite of the fact that he is one of the most loved and respected comedians in Ireland.

Certainly Frank did not gravitate to the comedy stage by a direct route, as he was first a musician playing the organ at St Joseph's Church, Mayfield. The day job was as an insurance official on the South Mall. 'Some evenings I played the piano as accompanist at charity concerts, and then at Sunday night concerts in venues, including theatres, around the city.'

Frank remembers with unconcealed good humour that the licensing laws of the time meant that there were just two places one could get a drink on a Sunday after 10.30 p.m. These were the old Opera House and a designated rowing club. There were ways to circumvent the law, since those with a distinct thirst could travel a requisite three miles from those venues and acquire a pint or two by claiming to the publican that a journey of three miles had indeed been undertaken.

Because of this restriction the Opera House was assured a full house each Sunday night, no matter the quality of the show on stage. Otherwise, it was a retreat to a boat club on the Marina, or a bike ride against a prevailing westerly on a dark winter's evening to the Anglers' Rest at the end of the Straight Road.

Frank recalls a theatre story of the time. One Sunday night in the AOH Hall there was a lady in full voice on stage in a rendition of that great favourite 'The Old Refrain'. When the singer came to the line, 'It was my mother taught me how to sing . . .', there was the unmistakable sound of a beer bottle falling from the grasp of its somewhat inebriated and emotional owner and a strangled voice was heard to say, 'She has a lot to answer for . . .'

The first time Frank played the piano in public was upstairs in the old CCYMS Hall in Castle Street. The piano was set quite close to the audience, front of stage. 'I knew that Chris Sheehan would be on just after the interval, so we met backstage. He told me that he was going to sing "When the Sergeant Major is On Parade".' Chris handed him the 'dots' (sheet music), but Frank said that he only played 'by ear'. 'Take the dots, boy,' said Chris. To please him, Frank took the music and placed it on the piano stand in front of him. 'Once I got the key I ignored the music sheet, but halfway through the song, an old lady in a shawl came over to the piano and, in a loud voice, declared, "Little boy, you have the music upside down."'

For all that, Frank's musical abilities were in demand and put to good use whenever the great James N. Healy began planning and rehearsing his next Nigel Hay production from the Gilbert and Sullivan repertoire. Frank acted as *répétiteur* at rehearsals and sometimes he would be in the orchestra for a show.

James N. put on a show in the Father Mathew Hall called *Memories of the Old Opera House*, including a tribute to 'The Warblers' of Danny Hobbs fame. 'I was in the orchestra and in some of the ensemble items on stage.'

Then James N. wrote his own show entitled *Himself.* It opened at the Opera House and then went on tour to California at the same time as the Southern Theatre Group had gone out with the John B. Keane plays, *Sive* and *The Year of the Hiker*, and *The Country Boy* by John Murphy.

Another time we toured the east coast with the *Percy French* show which James N. had also devised. We toured to New Jersey, Ocean City and Atlantic City.

On stage with James N. was Jacinta Mulcahy in a role that was later performed by Deirdre White. We played to mainly Irish American audiences and did extremely well. We also toured *Percy French* to the north of Ireland. What I found interesting was that audiences up there were in the main Protestant– Unionist. We did it in Derry and Percy French's two daughters, Ettie and Joan, met us afterwards.

The daughters of Percy French, Ettie and Joan, attended a performance of James N. Healy's devised show based on the songs and times of the composer. Also included are Deirdre White and Frank Duggan.
(© Private Collection)

In a Percy French song ('Come Back Paddy Reilly to Bally- jamesduff') there is reference to the Bridge of Finay. Frank is unlikely to forget it. On his way to the show, all the way from Cork, he got lost near the same bridge. The show was an after- dinner affair and Frank arrived, as he thought, with just ten minutes to spare, to learn that the show's starting time had been switched from 10 p.m. back to 9 p.m. – a fact that James N. had omitted to tell Frank. However, the audience had waited for Frank and the show went down well. Frank remembers:

> We stayed overnight and I drove James N. home to Cork the next morning. James was not feeling well so I drove him straight to the Bon Secours Hospital. James N., a true theatre legend, passed to his eternal reward without ever leaving hospital.
>
> James N. was a man who deserved more credit than he got from the public. Success in the States came to him late in life and it was a terrible pity that international acclaim did not come much earlier in his career. He had a fine, resonant voice and great stage presence. He was outstanding as Bull McCabe in *The Field*. He was a major presence in Cork for so many years.

In the little spare time from the office and his accompaniment gigs, Frank was writing scripts for those putting on amateur shows. This went to another level when the then manager of the Opera House, Bill Twomey, took two scripts from him for pantos in the late 1950s. In the same year Frank was musical director for the panto in the Father Mathew Hall. Later he would write scripts for the *Tops of the Town* and sketches for the Insurance Institute group.

Frank Duggan has fond memories of the *Slag* shows: 'They were ahead of their time. They were a new departure. Comedy in Cork then would have been fairly traditional sketches, like those used by Jimmy O'Dea, Jack Cruise in *Holiday Hayride*, and similar to those we were to use in *Summer Revels* much later. The *Slag* shows were pure satire and the writer Colum Fehily was wonderfully talented. His strength was his ability to see comedy in a political situation.'

Frank recalls those chance happenings in life that can change the course of a life, in the same way as does Michael Twomey. 'A friend of mine Bill O'Herlihy had joined Montrose from the *Examiner*. I gave Bill a monologue for *Newsbeat's* Frank Hall who, in turn, suggested that the piece would work better as a duologue.'

Frank Duggan and Michael Twomey worked on it. It really took off for the same TV audience who had already been convulsed with laughter at Miah's vox pop piece on the hazards of smoking.

So Frank, the musician who had wanted to make it as a performer on stage, first become a household name on national TV as a comedian. 'To this day, Michael Twomey maintains that we started at the top and worked our way down.'

Men of Mettle –Cha (Frank Duggan) and Friend at the County Hall, Cork.
(© Hatchell)

Initially the duo wrote their own scripts, since *Newsbeat* was a pot-pourri of different subjects. Later the format of the programme changed and was built around one central theme, so Frank Hall began writing their scripts for the show. 'They were very good and worked well. We would make some idiomatic adjustments but Frank Hall did not like us to do so. We were on *Newsbeat* and then *Hall's Pictorial Weekly* on a regular basis from 1969 to when it ended in the early 1980s. It was out of those somewhat haphazard and humble beginnings that Cha and Miah developed.'

Filming of the Cha and Miah sketch was done every Saturday morning for about three hours with the most popular backdrop being the Marina. Cha and Miah were welcomed in almost every county in the Republic, though Frank believes that they did miss Donegal, Monaghan and Louth in their travels. There were some hilarious moments then, on and off the stage, with some scary happenings.

Frank recalls being lost en route on several occasions. Invariably they picked the wrong person to show them the way to the hall where they were due to play that night. Quite often it was the classic case of being sent the wrong way for all the right reasons. Often precious minutes were lost as the 'helpful' guide would give lengthy instructions, only to change his or her mind and start all over again. However, the intrepid duo always managed to make the right venue on the right night.

One night they received an unusually short introduction to the stage. No big build-up as usual to create the right atmosphere and, not only that, but they found themselves locked into a room beside the stage. By the time they got on stage, there was not a sound, not a bleat of welcome. To make matters worse, just one mike was working; the other had collapsed when Frank had wrestled with it, as it had been pre-set for use with a saxophone. He almost did himself an injury in the process but it had to be abandoned and he had to share

Miah's mike. No mean feat when the two were in full flight with the repartee.

On another night Michael and Frank had driven up country and arrived just in time to get on with the show. There was no time to get something to eat, so they looked forward to having a sandwich at the venue afterwards. There was a problem. A large dog guarded the upstairs room where the food was available. Michael assured Frank that if they did not show fear they could get past the dog in safety. The dog stood up and snarled. The lads decided that they were not as hungry as they had first thought and drove home without their supper.

Frank says, 'Because of the positive TV exposure, we were in demand all over the country. We'd leave our places of work, travel to Sligo, Dublin or the midlands, do our act, and drive straight home to be up the next morning for another day at the office.'

Then there were the extra-special occasions. Remarkably, Cork's finest exports were not together when one of the most popular *Late Late Shows* of all time was screened at Montrose, with the greatest broadcaster in the history of the state, Gay Byrne, in the chair.

Frank has particularly vivid memories of that night in 1982 when Ireland was entertained royally by what was, in effect, the best line-up of Cork talent ever assembled for a TV show. On the guest panel that evening were Dublin 'exiles' Niall Toibín, Joe Lynch and Chris Curran, with Cork-based Dave McInerney, James N. Healy, Billa and Chris Sheehan.

In the audience were guest performers Paddy Comerford, Dan Coughlan, Mary Hegarty, Marie Twomey, Christy Morris and Donal Kenneally. Brothers Donal and George Crosbie delighted with their witty harmonies, delivered with impeccable timing.

That night Gay Byrne went amongst the audience to give a special welcome to the great Ignatius Comerford, definitive panto dame. When he was only thirty-four years of age, illness robbed us of his understated brilliance on the stage. That *Late Late* is still talked about and tapes of the show are collectors' items. It was a wonderful occasion and it went down a treat with the studio audience and viewers in homes all over Ireland. The show had that indefinable buzz about it. So great were the performances that one would have thought that the whole thing was a spontaneous and relaxed showcasing of real Cork talent. Not so as far as Frank Duggan is concerned.

'I was a nervous wreck, sick from sheer nerves. I had rehearsed with the Cork-based singers, Marie Twomey, Chris Sheehan, Donal Kenneally, Christy Morris, Dan Coughlan. Also, on my own, I went over and over the accompaniments. On top of that we had the Cha and Miah sketch, which was an insert tape as Michael Twomey was adjudicating elsewhere on the night of the *Late Late*.'

In the sketch Cha and Miah made out that they had not been invited and were not at all pleased with the powers that be in Donnybrook. In conclusion the miffed duo announced to the nation:

And from now on, we'll say,
We'll watch only Match of the Day,
On 'The Banks Of My Own Lovely Lee'

'I arrived at RTÉ about two hours before the show, but I couldn't get to a piano to rehearse. However, everything went very well on the night,' Frank recalls.

From their very first appearance Cha and Miah struck a

certain chord with viewers and their live audiences – even family pets were named Cha and Miah! Miah was always the dominant know-it-all, and Cha the 'God help us' character – the 'gob-daw', *óinseach* type with the hangdog countenance. He was apparently in awe of his more confident partner Miah, but scoring points when least expected, much to the chagrin of Miah. The inherent gifts evident in all their performances were good material, exquisite timing and perfect delivery. Frank says, 'Another bonus for us when we appeared outside of Cork County was the Cork accent itself. To everyone else's ears that accent was perfect in the context of humour.'

I wondered if Cha missed travelling with his pal to the halls of Ireland. Was it hard to let go? 'I think I miss it more than Michael. He is so involved directing and adjudicating. Unless the feeling is mutual about doing something, there is no pressure from me.'

Frank paid this tribute to Michael: 'He has that great ability to know what works in a sketch and what will go well. Whatever modicum of ability I had in putting comedy across to an audience, he certainly helped to develop it. He goes into tremendous detail. He also has a very even temperament. We've travelled thousands of miles as Cha and Miah and, while we might have had an occasional 'skirmish', we always remained great friends. We have never fallen out. Michael is never confrontational.'

Interestingly, Frank feels that Miah might not have been the best name for his comrade in comedy. 'Up the country it has been mis-pronounced and even members of the media got it wrong, with versions including Mee-ah and Mee-aw.'

Never seen on our screens now and missing from our stages except on special occasions, Cha and Miah made lives by De

Banks, the Shannon, Corrib, Liffey, Blackwater, Barrow, Nore and Suir brighter and infinitely more tolerable. They won a Jacobs Award for their TV appearances. They were jointly honoured a few years ago with the Cork Person of the Month Award. They filmed one of the Cha and Miah sequences for Frank Hall outside Cork County Hall, looking up at it and calculating how much they should charge for cleaning all the windows! Thereafter the two famous statues standing there were nicknamed Cha and Miah and are so called to this day.

Bench mark – Frank Duggan and Michael Twomey as Cork Persons Of The Month in May 2002, on the very bench where they addressed the nation in Halls Pictorial Weekly

It is true that Michael and Frank were not happy with their few panto appearances. 'We did two or three pantos in the mid-'70s. We worked with the likes of Noel V. Ginnity and Tony Kenny. We were cast as the Baron's henchmen. It did not work in the context of panto. I found it hard going. Entertaining children is a special skill. All the kids want to see is the dame chasing someone around the stage. We did not fit in to that set-up,' recalls Frank.

Frank was an ever-present in *Summer Revels* for twenty-one consecutive years. It was one of the most popular variety shows of all time. Things did not always go according to script, however. Frank remembers one scene when he was a gangster with fellow hoods Michael, Dave McInerney, Billa O'Connell and Paddy Comerford. They were to make their big entrance on stage, but Frank accidentally tripped on the curtain and all four ended in a heap on stage. The audience loved it.

A keen student of how and why humour works in different contexts, Frank goes back to his early days of listening to the radio.

> On radio it is the material and your timing. Subconciously I picked that up from radio over the years. Michael Twomey has a superb sense of timing. Then, for stage and TV, there had to be the visual element. It is the way Cha and Miah evolved over the years.
>
> Miah is the know-all, the wise one, and Cha is always impressed with Miah's knowledge. But now and again I come up with a little gem, but I do not realise that it is a gem. I wasn't the first Cha but when I settled into it I gave it my own personal interpretation.

I believe that, as with all great acts, Cha and Miah are simply incomparable. May there always be two stools and a bar counter for them, if they so wish, so that they can carry us on colourful flights of fancy and fun, away from this black and white world. They have hung up their flat caps, they have put away the long coats and appear now only on special occasions. We miss them. May they never leave that bench on De Banks.

Chapter 9
Playing the Game

Dan Coughlan

If Michael Twomey's mother did not want her darling son playing rugby in Pres, Dan Coughlan's parents were content to see their boy excel on the field of play. He was the true all-rounder, performing at the highest level in many codes, but, in time, he would be attracted to the world of theatre.

Dan, as a Presentation College boy, was their star out-half at junior and senior level. He loved water polo and remembers playing a game with his team, Dolphin, at Limerick City quays. One goal was tied to the rudder of a ship and the other to the quay wall. 'There was more oil than water that day in the Shannon, but we still played,' laughs Dan. Dolphin were Munster champions two years running.

As a member of the famous Western Rovers soccer team, he played in an FAI Minor Cup against Home Farm. They played a 1–1 draw in the final at Donnybrook in Dublin. In the replay the Cork lads were expected to win well, but went down 5–1 in the Mardyke.

Dan was also an outstanding hurler and footballer, but because he had played in a cricket match, he was 'banned' from playing with the Barrs. Dan recalls his mild-mannered father telling some club mentors what he thought of that 'ban' when they met in the Lough Tavern one evening. Dan and his pals, Noel Noonan, Joe Sullivan and Dave Geary, were still only in Pres when they won Munster Junior Cup medals with Highfield.

An appropriately bluff and hearty performance was how one critic saw Dan Coughlan's playing of the retired army general in Don't Tell Father
(© private collection)

Dan joined Cork Con and played with the Temple Hill side for a few years, but already the world of theatre was, as Dan puts it, 'starting the rot'. So Dan, who might have worn the red jersey of Cork or the green for Ireland in rugby, was to have his finest hours, not on the playing fields of Ireland, but on theatre stages, home and away.

Der Breen and Dan Donovan were the driving forces behind the Presentation Theatre Guild. When Pres College on the Mardyke was building a new hall on the Western Road side of the new college, Der ensured that it would have a raised stage area at one end. The Guild became All-Ireland Amateur Drama Champions when they were crowned at the National finals at

Father Mathew Hall in Dublin for their production of *Journey's End*.

Later Dan gave a memorable performance in the Guild's production of *The Queen and the Rebels*, with Abby Scott, Charlie Hennessy, Lorna Daly and Michael Twomey in the cast. It reached the All-Ireland finals in Athlone, but the winners that year were the Listowel Players with a new play, *Sive*.

Dan recalls Guild productions of *Murder in the Cathedral*, *Thunder Rock* and *Julius Caesar*. There was also the odd farce such as *Tons of Money*, which had a fine cast including Dan Donovan, Mary O'Carroll, Brendan Fitzgerald, Myra Spillane, Redmond Burke, Stella Sheehan, Nan McHenry, Ted Sullivan and John Harrington.

Journey's End deserves special mention as it was to set new production standards. The manager at the Opera House in 1946 was the great John Daly. He had a blank week in his programming, so he approached Der Breen about the Guild's production of *Journey's End*.

It was agreed that this amateur group would make the giant leap on to the big stage of the old Opera House. Daly was to take over the direction, with Der Breen in the lead. The cast also included Redmond Burke, Joe O'Sullivan and Dan Donovan, with Dan Coughlan as the young soldier. Dan says:

> I remember going to rehearsals and coming home shattered. The director pointed to the play's homosexual undercurrent. In my innocence I had no idea what the man was talking about.
>
> The director brought in the Irish army for the final scene when a German shell wipes us out. Paddy Buckley was stage-manager and the command would

be, 'Number one', which would be the cue for the sound of small rifle fire from on high. 'Number two' signalled machine-gun fire. Then there were the maroons, a sort of hand-grenade. Two of these would be sealed in tin dustbins and exploded with an almighty bang. When we came to take our bows each night the place was covered in smoke, we could hardly see the audience.

Each night the army people would pile into a lorry with their guns and ammo and head back to Collins Barracks to return again the next night.

One night we thought there had been an accident when John Daly could not take a bow, as his face was covered in blood. It turns out he had had a massive nosebleed – whether it was the tension of the whole thing we never found out. He was a great character. That week we had the worst possible weather with ice and snow, but the audiences still came. We learned an awful lot from John Daly. He had a very deep knowledge of theatre.

Dan appeared in a string of productions at the Father Mathew Hall. He was coping with all the problems associated with trying to balance the demands of marriage, new home, day job, against the pressures of getting to a theatre each evening for a curtain at 8 p.m. 'I'd find myself making a business call in Charleville at five o'clock. Then it was a dash back to Cork for a bite to eat and another race in to the city to the theatre. James Stack, as director, knew what the audience liked and he gave it to them. We'd do about two comedies in a year.'

A contemporary of Dan's was Michael McAuliffe. He had

been with Father O'Flynn and then joined James Stack's classes at the old School of Music. More than thirty years later Michael would pay homage to his former teacher, Father O'Flynn, when he adapted Richard O'Donoghue's biography of O'Flynn, *Like A Tree Planted* (Gill & Son, 1967) for the stage. He called the play quite simply *Flynnie.*

Flynnie was a remarkable hit. It ran first at the old Cork Arts Theatre and then transferred to the Opera House. The life of Father O'Flynn – soul brother to northsiders for twenty-six years – was told in a series of brilliantly witty sketches. Theatre critic Mary Leland described *Flynnie* as a 'rich evocation of Cork life, joyous, raucous, devout and imbued with that kind of simple humour which, while transcending locality, remains utterly indigenous'.

In the Cork Arts Theatre Annual Awards, adjudicated by media theatre critics, the play won: Best Director and Best Actor for Michael McAuliffe; Best Supporting Actor for Dan Coughlan; Best Actress for Mon Murphy; and Best Lighting for Liam Ward. The awards were a way of recognising local talent on stage and in production categories. They were also an effective means to ensure that there was some continuity of review and they maintained interest in local productions over each theatrical season. They should be revived now that the splendid new Cork Arts Theatre is up and running. The excellent *Flynnie* cast included Mary Foley, Anne Marie Cotter and Kevin Sheehan.

The actual award citation for *Flynnie* said it all, with regard to Michael McAuliffe and his cast: 'For the courage to hold an idea, to give it shape and life by bringing it to the stage, for gathering the perfect cast who played together with the sustained brilliance which only veterans can command.'

The thousands who saw Dan Coughlan perform on stage will recall his appearances in a string of musicals in which he usually played the comedic character. Dan never considered that he had a good voice but, as with all good actors, he managed to deliver his lines with that kind of reassuring confidence that endeared him to his audiences.

Dan Coughlan as Crowdle Coen in No Home Tomorrow
(© Liam O'Connell)

He was Blinky Bill in *The Belle of New York*, with T. A. Sheridan Moffitt directing and with a set by the late Frank Sanquest who made a remarkable contribution to Cork theatre for decades. The cast featured Josephine Cahill, Mary Cagney, Ettie Jenkins, James N. Healy, Kevin O'Regan, Tommy Dynes, Pat Cagney, Billy Williams, Charlie Blair, Chris Sheehan, Kay Buckley, Cyril Neville, and Ken and Robert Campbell. Choreography was by Nancy Wine.

The year was 1950 and November saw a production of *Show Boat*, with Josephine O'Hagan as Magnolia, Kevin O'Regan as Cap'n Andy and Herbert Wellwood as Gaylord Ravenal. Dan played Frank, joined by Terry Cashman (Joe), Robert Campbell (Pete), Ged O'Donovan Reid (Julie), Cecilia Maguire (Ellie) and Gordon Blair as Vallon. Producer was Quintin Golder, décor by Frank Sanquest. Nancee Cavanagh was responsible for the dance sequences with P. A. Buckley, stage director.

At the Father Mathew Hall Dan was Phantis in the 1958

production of *Utopia Limited*, directed by James N. with a very strong cast, including: Norman Butler, Pierre Blanc, Gerry Rearden, John De Foubert, Fred South, Cyril Neville, Gordon Blair, David McInerney, Richard Greenham, Michael Herley, Mary Cullinane, Roberta Fitzgibbon, Siobhán O'Brien, Ronnie O'Shaughnessy, Flora Kerrigan, Dom O'Callaghan and Marjorie Heffernan.

When a disastrous fire gutted the old Opera House in November 1955, Father Mathew Hall became the main venue for productions. One unique offering that grew out of that disaster was the Gilbert and Sullivan Group presentation of *Memories of the Opera House*. It recalled the good old days in the Emmet Place institution. A programme note for the evening of 15 February 1959 said it all: 'A programme deliberately designed to bring tears of sad remembrance of the old theatre to your eyes and send you rushing down to Emmet Place tomorrow with a lump of sentiment in your throat and a load of money in your pocket for the organiser (Mr Frank O'Leary), Opera House Building Fund, Emmet Place, Cork.' Although there may not have been tears that night, the show did feature a satire with the remarkable title 'When Bananas Grow on Gaslamps in Blackpool'.

The *Cork Examiner* drove the renovation campaign forward with tireless zeal, led by Stephen Coughlan and Crichton Healy. Crichton, many believe, remains unsurpassed in passion and depth of knowledge on matters relating to the performance arts, particularly theatre and film.

Stephen applied himself to the restoration programme with the same infectious enthusiasm which marked his drive to put Cork on the world map with its own airport. These two were supported by Donal Crosbie who later became (as had his father, George, before him) a director and chairman of the Opera House. Donal was for all things Cork, but his love of the Opera House was apparent in his every waking hour. He made no apology for this almost obsessive zeal – his enthusiasm, and that of others like him, kept the theatre doors open.

Donal Crosbie, Chris Curran, Neil Toibin and Harry Anthony in the old Examiner *offices printing floor.*
(© Irish Examiner)

Even when Donal was very ill, he attended (in the company of Norma, his wife) a performance by the National Ballet Company, such was his concern to promote the cause of theatrical companies. And, during his time as Editorial Director at the *Examiner*, he always strove to ensure that the paper consistently promoted and backed Cork theatre. When he died, the Opera House and Cork lost a true champion. Another Crosbie, Ted, was to become the driving force of Opera 2005, one of the more tangible artistic legacies of Cork's tenure as European Capital of Culture in 2005.

However, in the years from 1955 to 1965, when the dear old Opera House was still a building site, many venues around the city would be pressed into use to fill the void left in the theatrical life of the city. Dan Coughlan reflects on the situation: 'The Father Mathew Hall was fine for plays with a cast maximum of eight, but musicals needed greater on- and off-stage space. There could be forty on stage with a chorus.'

Step up once more Dan's old Pres colleague, Der Breen, who was manager of the Palace Cinema on MacCurtain Street. Der, for all his association with the founding of Cork Film Festival, was a theatre man at heart, so they were pushing at an open door. Cork Operatic Society presented *Oklahoma* and *Annie Get Your Gun* in the Palace, and a production of *Finian's Rainbow*, with Dan as Finian McLonergan. This last was actually the World Amateur Première of A. Y. Harburg and Burton Lane's musical comedy. Production was by Dan Donovan, with musical direction by Sheridan Moffitt. Some interesting cast names included Milo O'Shea (playing Óg), Fidelma Murphy, Agnes and Bob Carlile and Cherry Hutson of the Cork Ballet Company.

Cork Operatic Society, as with all companies, could not continue to present major musicals every few months, but it could tap into the remarkably varied talents of its members. *Operantics*, a show from that era, was not so much a musical as a revue-style production, using lyrics from Operatic Society members set to well-known tunes, pop and classical, of the time.

In the first *Operantics* at the Father Mathew Hall there were eighteen sketches in all. Tony Murphy's fashion show take-off, 'Modes for Morons', with Lorna Daly as Commere, had the audience in stitches. Dan Coughlan and Mon Murphy were a hit as they followed the fashion of courting couples around the world. The cast also included Michael Twomey, Charlie Hennessy, Vass Anderson, Siobhán O'Brien, Abby Scott, Marie Twomey, Mary Keating, Aida O'Flynn, Rosarii McNamara, Bill Callanan, Billy Williams, Eileen Forest and Eric O'Leary. *More Operantics* followed at the Palace, with Nancy O'Donovan, Harry Wallace, Billy Newman and Liam O'Connell included in the revue team.

Dan Coughlan wonders to this day how some of the Cork Operatic Society's productions ever reached the stage, there was so much fun in their rehearsal. He recalls the sketch called the 'Operantics Film Festival' (1960), which was set at the airport as the various personalities arrived for the Festival. Dan was to carry a tea chest from stage left to right. Wonderful theatre man Harry Fitzgerald Smith was stage-manager, and he suggested that he would set it centre stage to cut Dan's journey by half. What Dan did not know was the crew had nailed the box to the stage. It would not budge despite Dan's best efforts.

Again, in *Finian's Rainbow*, Dan (as Finian) had to hand over to another character the crock of gold that was placed under the log at centre stage. 'I went over to it and saw that someone had put in it three sixteen-pound weights used to secure the struts around the stage. As I struggled to lift the crock, one of the round weights took off and was rolling towards the orchestra pit. Milo O'Shea who was on stage spotted it and averted disaster by putting his foot on the weight.'

In the second of the *Operantics* shows, topics tackled and set to music included 'Lament for the Bona Fides', 'Fertility' and 'Thoughts on Men'. They were all given the *Operantics* treatment to hilarious effect. Members of the company included Mr Music himself, Joe Hayes, Pat Fleming (former manager of the Opera House and now front-of-house manager at the Everyman Palace), Loretta McNamara (formerly of Mercier Press) and Irene Comerford, a valued member of Cork and Kinsale casts over the years. Scripts were by Tony Murphy, George Crosbie, Vass Anderson, Michael Twomey and Charlie Hennessy.

Although primarily comedians, Dan Coughlan, James N. Healy, Michael Twomey, Dave McInerney, Tony Hegarty, Paddy Comerford and many others were so versatile that there was continual movement between theatrical genres. In 1959 Dan was Mike Glavin in the play *Sive*, which made Listowel's John B. Keane one of the best-known and loved playwrights in Ireland. John B. drew his inspiration from the wellspring of his native Kerry. *Sive* turned the Irish theatre world on its head and eventually disturbed one of its most sacred cows, the Abbey Theatre, which initially rejected the play.

One critic, B. L., was not as impressed as the rest of the country – including the audience in Clonmel – when he reviewed the performance there. He spoke of an 'immature work' and made reference to a 'Noreen Bawn repertoire' of the travelling tent shows. However, he recognised 'depth and feeling' in the performances of Dan Coughlan as Sive's Uncle Mike Glavin and of Michael McAuliffe as Liam Scuab, the young lover.

Sive was a strange phenomenon in Ireland but everyone was talking about it, including theatrical luminaries like Stanley Illsley and Leo McCabe – suddenly an unknown writer had had his play about a young girl being married off to an old man performed brilliantly and to much acclaim, first by an amateur company from Keane's own town, Listowel, and then, with sold-out success, by Southern Theatre Group in Cork.

The Olympia audience saw it first on 16 November 1959, with Dan Donovan directing, and starring Dan Coughlan as Mike Glavin, Nora Relihan as Mena, Kay Healy as Nanna, Margaret Dillon as Sive, James N. Healy as Thomasheen Seán Rua, Michael McAuliffe as Liam Scuab, Charles Ginnane as Seán Dota, Tom Vesey as Pats Bocock and Charlie Kelleher as Carthalawn.

John B. went on to make a wonderfully earthy contribution to comedy theatre, much of it based on his 'Letters' newspaper column, including the 'Matchmaker' series. If great minds to madness are near allied (to paraphrase the Bard), then John B.'s plays always had that detectable seam of humour running through them, leavening the dark drama at their core.

James Stack was a giant influence on many of Dan's contemporaries. Stacky, it appears, made the difference between success and failure on the commercial stage. Those who went on to make their mark in theatre credit the man as the one who influenced their subsequent work on stage. His drama classes in the old School of Music were the nursery where the artistic seeds were first germinated.

Dan always considered that Stack was a master of popular theatre and appeared in a succession of Stack's hit productions, particularly at the Father Mathew Hall. I have yet to read an adverse review of his work on stage, but one particular note speaks volumes about the teacher and pupil relationship. It followed the opening night of John McCann's *Give Me A Bed Of Roses*, with Dan Coughlan as Bill, leader of the Yellow Tigers Dance Band: 'The ease and assurance of your performance charmed everyone. A grand job, Dan. It was a pleasure to work with you. Sincere congratulations and thanks, Jim [Stack].' That cast included: Lorraine Jones, Bill Mahony, Mon Murphy, Michael McAuliffe, Chris Whitnell, Siobhán O'Brien, Der Donovan and Vass Anderson.

Another 1960 triumph was the Irish première of *Not in the Book* by Arthur Watkyn, with Dave McInerney as Police Inspector Malcolm, Pat Fenton as Timothy Gregg and Dan as Colonel Barstow. *Easy Money* and *Tons of Money*, directed by Rex Archer, followed in 1961 at the same venue. *Easy Money* was a particular triumph for Michael McAuliffe with Lorna Daly, Philip Stafford and young Margaret Newman as the *enfant terrible* in a house expecting easy money from the pools. Rex Archer again directed Dan and Kevin Sheehan in a great production of the E. E. Evans comedy, *The Wishing Well*.

Cork has been blessed with a succession of fine directors and actors, but good writers for the stage have been thin on the ground by comparison. There was a real buzz of anticipation then when John Power handed his script of *As Some Tall Cliff* to James Stack for a world première at the Father Mathew Hall.

James gathered around him a strong cast of Bill Mahony, Lorraine Jones, Dan Coughlan, Abby Scott, John McCarthy, Paddy Cotter, Mary O'Donovan, Bob Carlile Jnr, Jack Riordan, Maeve Delaney, Mildred Hassett and Sean MacCarthaigh. It was a home triumph for the writer who also excelled as an astute observer and historian of the Cork hurling world. *Don't Tell Father*, again directed by Rex Archer, brought Dan Coughlan and Kevin Sheehan together as Sir Mathew Carr and General Barclay.

Just a few months after the new Opera House opened its doors in 1965, Dan was back with James Stack directing his portrayal of Guardsman Arthur Crisp in John Dighton's *Who Goes There?* (also starring Lorna Daly, Jim Queally, Pat Fenton, David McInerney, Donal O'Donovan and Mary O'Donovan). Dan recalls, 'Lorna had that wonderful sense of timing, but above all she was able to go inside a role and those playing opposite her were able to work off this inner strength and their performances were enhanced.'

James Stack thought highly of Dan as an actor, but was not impressed with one aspect of his interpretation of Guardsman Crisp. Lorna was Lady Alex Cornwall and in one scene this unlikely couple were sitting on a bench. Lady Alex was impressing on Crisp that, because of the obvious social divide, there could not be anything remotely romantic between them. Dan decided that he might win the audience over by flicking at his busby headgear every now and again. Every time he did so, there was a peal of laughter. After the scene director Stack was waiting in the wings and simply said, 'Don't do that again.' The director was not for the easy laugh if it meant the leading lady in the play was being upstaged.

In Dan's view, at the period when he was embarking on his theatrical career, the great comedienne of the stage was Ettie Jenkins. Ettie was Mamie in the 1950 production of *The Belle of New York*. 'Ettie was a natural, the Rosaleen Linehan of her time. Others would follow such as Mon Murphy and Mary O'Donovan who also had that essential comic timing.'

Dan Coughlan was back on the musical stage when he played Max in Cork Operatic Society's *The Sound of Music* (1970). Again Dan was the conduit of what fun there can be in a musical that has as its dramatic backdrop the Nazis' burgeoning rampage of power in Europe.

When I spoke to Dan about his time on stage, I got the

distinct impression that his favourite role had been that of Nathan Detroit in Cork Operatic Society's production of *Guys and Dolls* on the Opera House stage in April 1971. David McInerney was Sky Masterson, Paddy Comerford was Nicely-Nicely Johnson, with Maura Dowling as Sarah Brown, and Mon Murphy as Miss Adelaide.

Cool Dude: Dan Coughlan as Nathan Detroit in Guys and Dolls
(© private collection)

Jeff Kidner, Dan Coughlan, Liam O'Connell and Mary Healy played multi-roles in J. P. Donleavy's *Fairytales of New York* (design by Frank Fitgerald, direction by Michael McCarthy) as part of an Everyman season.

Critics Geraldine Neeson and Bobby O'Donoghue agreed that the Collins Musical Society's production of *Land of Smiles* at the Cork Opera House in 1973 was its best. Directed by Harry Bogan, Brian Donlan from the Glyndebourne Company was Prince Sou Chong, Mary Brennan was Lisa, Jean Cousins was Mi, Noel Murphy was Lieutenant Westhof. The show also starred Elaine Stevens as Countess Roheim and Dan as Chi-Fu, with musical direction by Commandant R. B. Kealy

Dan starred in *The Wizard of Oz,* directed by Jimmy Bellchamber and his version of this classic musical at the Opera House in Easter 1973 stays with me to this day. It was one of those, all too rare, occasions when an evening of theatre creates a special bond between those on stage and the audience. As we sat in the stalls on that magical evening of theatre, my eldest son (then seven) insisted on sitting on my lap with his arms wrapped around my neck as he watched the most endearing musical comedy adventure story unfold on stage.

I wondered if the whole thing was too much for him, but I need not have worried. There was little sleep later that night while my children – like the others who had been in the audience, no doubt – lived again the adventures of Dorothy, played beautifully in this production by Colette Good. Dan as the Lion, David McInerney as Tin Man and Paddy Comerford as Scarecrow were scene-stealers, as were Rachel Burrows as the Sorceress and Mon Murphy as the Wicked Witch.

The musical director was John Murphy of the School of Music and the shimmering costumes and stunning sets were by Pat Murray. Critics of the time, Flor Dullea, Bobby O'Donoghue and Jean Sheridan, were unanimous in giving the show top marks. One programme note is worthy of mention: 'Bicycles by courtesy of Bridewell Garda Station of Cornmarket Street'!

Former Pres boys Dan Donovan, Dan Coughlan and Michael Twomey had their dramatic grounding with the Guild, and later with James Stack. They put it to good use in what was considered to be one of the finest productions of the Arthur Miller classic *Death of a Salesman*, which opened at the Everyman Playhouse in Father Mathew Street and transferred to the Opera House in Emmet Place.

Brilliantly directed by Michael Twomey, it had Dan Donovan as Willie Loman and Dan Coughlan as his neighour Charlie, with excellent design by Frank Fitzgerald. Geraldine Neeson described Dan Coughlan's performance as 'one of the best pieces of sincere, controlled acting'. This was another example of the sheer versatility of this band of artistes – Michael, Dan Donovan and Dan Coughlan proved themselves, yet again, equally at home in works as diverse as those by Miller, Keane, Hammerstein or Loesser.

Michael and Dan Coughlan were in a Feydeau farce, *The Gamecock*, a Theatre of the South production, which featured a show-stopping performance from another Pres product, Ber Power as Picot, and was directed by the Australian actor–director Peter O'Shaughnessy.

Ber Power directed the Everyman Playhouse production of Kenneth Horne's *Trial and Error*, which was a real Easter treat. It also marked the return of the Playhouse from exile at The Maltings to the Father Mathew Street Theatre after its makeover had been completed. The cast featured Maureen Fox, Michael Twomey, Dan Coughlan, Elaine Stevens, Mon Murphy, Gerry McLoughlin and Joss Cahill.

The 1980s, and another decade in showbiz for Dan Coughlan who reprised Max in the Cork Opera House production of *The Sound of Music*, with direction by Larry Oaks. Brid Hartnett was Maria opposite Philip Bond as Baron Von Trapp. Sheila O'Brien returned to her 1970 role of Mother Abbess. Dan always claimed that he could not sing, but those who saw him on RTÉ's *Late Late* in 1982, as well as starring in a string of musicals, would disagree. As with all good actors, his projection and timing more than made up for any vocal deficiency.

In the 1990s Dan Coughlan was completing fifty years on stage in Cork. He appeared in Feedback's fine stage adaptation of Flann O'Brien's *Thirst*, directed by Pat Talbot. Dan was a member of Fianna Dum in Tony Doherty's remarkable satire *GUBU 2*.

Dan is married to Helen Lannin, daughter of Joe Lannin, a member of the famous Warblers group. Helen also appeared on the musical stage. They love to spend some time in Crosshaven where Coastal Arts has presented some very lively theatre with the artistic support of Dan. The boy who had the sporting world at his educated feet became a man and combined his day job on the commercial road with a lifetime on the boards, rather than on the sporting field. He made the right choice. Cork theatre-goers should thank the heavens that he did so.

Chapter 10
The One and Only Billa

Billa O'Connell

Good comedy always travels well and easily. Billa O'Connell, considered by many to be the ultimate panto dame in Cork, has retired from the local stage but is still known and loved nationally for his TV appearances on programmes such as *Up for the Match* on the eve of All-Ireland hurling finals.

Billa was already a national star when those not blessed as Corkonians by birth got their first taste of some vintage comedy from the 'real capital' on Gay Byrne's now famous Cork *Late Late* in 1982. Billa told the hilarious story about the Cork family celebrating a son's return from work in Fords factory in Dagenham. 'Da sang and the dog howled in the yard!' Gay Byrne had decided that he had so much fun on a visit to Cork, when he had been entertained by local artistes, that he would have them come to his *Late Late* studio in Donnybrook and release them on the unsuspecting viewers of his hugely popular show. It was the move of a master. Billa and a host of stars, all laying claim to the Cork connection, made it one of the most talked-about *Late Lates* of all time. It was just another performance for Billa, who for decades before and after was the biggest box office attraction in Cork comedy theatre.

Billa was the one that young and old wanted to see and they flocked in their thousands each year to the Panto to catch their favourite in dress-up mode, complete with handbag, as he spurned the advances of the Baron baddie, routed his henchmen and made sure the principal boy was suitably attentive to this dame's daughter. Down all the years Billa simply *was* panto in Cork and children who are adults now recall with fondness their first experience of comedy theatre delivered by its star.

But one foul November night in 1955, Billa saw his plans for the future incinerated by the fire that ravaged the old Opera House:

> We were rehearsing for the panto, *Sleeping Beauty*, upstairs in the Opera House. James Stack was directing and I was sitting on a large hamper-style basket. I noticed there was smoke coming, as I thought, from the hamper. Then we could hear manager Bill Twomey ringing the fire brigade. Paddy Cotter said to Stacky that we'd better finish rehearsals and James said: 'Let the fire brigade investigate and we'll come back again.'
>
> We came out and we stood where the Christy Ring Bridge is now. I stood next to Seán Riordan. The building was ablaze. I said to myself that it would only be a shell in the morning. Everybody knows where they were when Kennedy was shot; every Cork man, woman and child knows where they were when the Opera House went on fire.

There was a woman standing in Emmet Place. She was very 'pound-notish' and was heard to say, 'I do hope they save the School of Art.' Another voice was heard: 'Era, f**k the School of Art.'

The old Opera House was a special part of the city. It was the same as Father Mathew's statue. It meant so much to people.

Billa had a very practical and understandable reason for wanting the old Opera House to survive the fire:

That time there were no credit unions, no hire purchase. Nell, my wife, and myself had our eyes on a suite of furniture for our sitting room. It was in Roches Stores. I could describe it to you this very minute. I was looking forward to making the price of it in a six-week run of the pantomime. On the night the old Opera House went on fire, I was home very late. I happened to look out the front bedroom window and saw that red glow still in the sky. I called Nell to see it. 'That's the aurora borealis,' she said. 'Aurora borealis?' says I. 'That's our sitting room suite gone up in smoke!'

I hadn't a bob. However, there was talk of bringing the *Sleeping Beauty* to the AOH Hall after the loss of the Opera House. Now very few people know this, but the AOH also went on fire that year. There was a jinx on that panto surely.

I can remember one morning sitting into my bread van and someone shouted to me that the AOH had a fire. I drove over to Morrison's Island and there was the AOH, which, after the firemen had finished, was just pools of water. That year was out and gone for me as far as pantos were concerned.

Mon Murphy and Billa O'Connell in panto mode
(© private collection)

Billa spoke about his entry into the manic world of panto.

> In the late '40s there had been a brilliant show called *Up Cork!* with Ignatius Comerford. I'm convinced to this day if Ignatius had not suffered a stroke, that he would have been another Barry Fitzgerald. He'd have made it big time in Hollywood.
>
> He was known as the dame, but he was a very versatile man. In straight theatre he was in *The Whip Hand* and he was in *The Winslow Boy*. My wife Nell's sister, Maureen, was his bridesmaid when he married. He was on top of the world. Himself and his wife

were living in Dunbar Street next to the Church. They were buying a house in Maryville in Blackrock when he got the stroke.

Up Cork! was, as one might expect from the title, pure Cork. Produced by MacBrien who was Finbarr McCarthy and Michael O'Brien combined, *Up Cork!* was a massive hit with audiences. It was done in revue style, with one theme running through it. Bob Carlile, Paddy Cotter, Sean White, Anne Brennan, Tadgh O'Leary and Mary Cronin were in the cast with the McTeggart Dancers. When Ignatius became ill and could not continue as the dame in *Up Cork!*, Billa recalls the moment when he was asked to take over the role.

> I was rehearsing for a play with James Stack in Father Mathew Hall. It was a Sunday morning. A deputation from the AOH came in the side door and asked me to take the role in the panto. I was honoured.
>
> I never considered I'd replace Ignatius because no one could do that. But I was thrilled to be dame in a series which was so popular when you consider that one *Up Cork!* ran for sixteen weeks, seven nights week.
>
> Not easy when you consider we had to work by day for those four months. The shortest run for an *Up Cork!* was nine weeks at the AOH. When we finished our run in Cork, we'd tour to nearly every hall in Munster. We'd do three nights in Bantry, in Cobh, in Bandon.

Billa has always had a great ballad voice. 'Myself and Bob Carlile would really milk it, appearing to hesitate about singing 'Silver Threads Among The Gold', but we always did and they loved it.'

Billa had truly found his voice in the *Up Cork!* shows. 'I was in Thompsons Bakery for seven pounds a week. I was working at night in the AOH for nine pounds a week. That was big money then, even if it was for seven nights a week. I was a man with a young family and the extra bobs were brilliant as a bob was a bob then.'

I asked Billa about the pressures of performance, particularly on such long runs in a revue-style show like *Up Cork!* 'I'd be as nervous on the last night as I was on the first but then I'd have a blinder. Once I got on stage I'd be grand. When I'd go home after a good night like that, I found it very hard to come down from that high. I'd put on the telly, and I saw a thousand John Wayne cowboy pictures as I tried to relax. It took its toll. Over fifty-one years, I did thirty-five pantos.'

I asked Billa if there was an irritability factor. 'I would get irritable before a show at home and in the theatre. The advice was to let me alone. Remember I was in the Opera House for three months of the year. I'd do panto for six weeks and then *Summer Revels* for another six weeks. *Revels* ran for twenty-one years. It ran each year from the end of August. I'd be down in Rosscarbery with my wife and children before rehearsals started and I'd be slipping away round the corner with a script in my hand. Happily I survived it.'

Billa loves the freedom now but he admits that he would still love to be able to do the shows like in the old days.

I know that I would get to the theatre and have a

blinder, but at my age I'm not taking that chance any more. I want the public, but my family, God bless them, know what's good for me.

I recall one night I was thrilled how well a panto performance had gone. I came home and I did not get to sleep until about five in the morning. I had a matinee the following day and a show that night again. That was Saturday night, so I had a show on Sunday and it was back to work on Monday. In those days for the first fortnight of the run there were two shows daily and my own children were on holidays but I could not be with them.

But, I do have the loveliest memories of those days and I loved when the children came up to me. Some of those children were in the Tiny Tots and they recall now what happy memories we have of those times on stage.

Christmas was tough, particularly when we opened on St Stephen's Day. When I'm learning a script I have to have it exact – every word, every line, down to the *seimhús* and the fadas.

My wife Nell and family would hardly see me for two months and remember rehearsals would start in the last week in November. My father only lived two doors above me here in the Lough. We were in *Up Cork!* for so many weeks and then we took it on tour. He came down to my house on Spy Wednesday and he saw my car in the drive. He wanted to know if I was sick, because he was so unused to seeing me at home.

For all that, I have no complaints. I did a panto in 1999 that ran into 2000. No regrets, they were great years and I'm very grateful for them.

I wonder if Billa and his colleagues, who shone on stage over those fifty or more years, really know how much they meant to audiences. That golden age of comedy theatre will never be repeated, so there is all the more reason to record and salute their achievements. The city and county needed a boost, as did the rest of the country. Jobs were in short supply; those that existed paid poorly; and, for decades, live theatre – be it revue or panto – was the only escape from a grey world.

Billa's association with the *Swans* goes back to their very foundation in the Father O'Leary Hall. 'I did two shows: *The Swans of the Lough* and *The Swans of the Lee*. At the time the Glen Hall was just built in Blackpool, so the title was changed to *The Swans of the Glen*. We brought *The Swans of the Lee* into Father Mathew Hall because Father Honorius OFM Cap asked me if we'd help out with fund-raising for the Trinity Church roof. I thought initially that it was only a night but it ran for a month. We nearly put on the roof ourselves.'

Getting an earful – Billa O'Connell and Paddy Comerford
(© private collection)

Billa played in Wembley Hall. Father Michael Cleary was to do a show there but he was unable to make it, so promoter Neilus O'Connell from Limerick asked Billa if he would act as compère.

> There were three and a half thousand in the hall. It was the start of Ireland Week. When I got there, I was given no running order. By the time the show was due to start, I had sorted out the show with the production crew. At the end of a great evening, they brought up the Wembley lights for me as a gesture of appreciation. I sang Mother Macree. There was a big man in the third row and the tears were running down his face.
>
> That night Foster and Allen were top of the bill and there was Billa in number two, which was to have been Father Cleary's spot. When nobody was looking, I took down my name from the door and I have the sign to this very day.

Also on the bill were the Shaskeen, Red Hurley and Jim McCann.

As Michael Twomey has said, Billa must be one of the most 'manly' dames in the history of panto. The avid Barrs clubman was always the man who dressed as a woman on stage. It is interesting to hear him talk about costuming when he is in panto dame mode. He would never go on stage if there was a ladder in the silk stockings, even though the ample dress covered all.

> Between matinee and evening shows, I'd park my car up by the Bridewell Garda Station. After the matinee

I'd go to six [o'clock] Mass in St Augustine's and then collect my sandwiches from the car to head down to the theatre again. It gave me such satisfaction to see coaches from all over Munster who had come to see the panto. Children would be passing me on the footpath, no idea as to who I was, but I could feel their excitement. I was often tempted to say, 'Hold on children, the show can't start without us.' I never did.

I remember one night after the show it was very foggy. I saw a woman and child behind the Opera House building. As I passed the mother pointed out that I was the man who played the dame. I learned that they had driven in from Millstreet on such a horrible night. I asked them if they had ever been backstage. They had not, so I brought them inside and sat the child in Cinderella's coach. That child 'sailed' out of the Opera House. I don't know if she remembers that evening, but I do. It gave me great satisfaction to see her so happy in that Cinderella coach.

Michael Twomey asked Billa if he would be a guest artiste in *Summer Revels*, which was spawned by the *Tops of the Town* shows. Billa agreed and was a headliner not for a few weeks, but for twenty-one years. Now, that's show business.

Michael Twomey and myself were a kind of team. He said to me that we'd bring in the millennium and when we got to 2001, I decided to call it a day. I had retired from the day job in Beamish and Crawford. Around Christmas, to this very day, I still feel I should be in a theatre.

I felt that there was a move away from the traditional panto. I saw a panto in the Opera House with Cinderella heading for the ball in a rocket ship. That was a mortal sin in my book. The story has to be told as it was written for children. One year there was a *Babes in the Wood* at the Palace and two adults played them. It should have been children playing those roles. I'm not knocking anyone, but I'm all for tradition. Michael Twomey and producers 'MacBrien' were all for tradition too. I still go to pantos, but I like to slip in for the matinee.

I reminded Billa of the night a little child stopped the show and put Dame Billa in his place.

It was the standard scene where I'd slip into bed and

It's In The Bag: Billa O'Connell brings the house down
(© private collection)

say, 'Nighty, night' to the children. Then I'd say, 'I love you.' Out of the darkness came a little voice: 'You never said your prayers.' I got out of bed and apologised to the child. I never got into that bed again without saying my prayers.

One year Paddy Comerford and myself were Ugly Sisters. We were heading off to the ball. I had just wiped the floor with Cinderella, telling her to get out of our way as I worked stage left. Paddy could not resist it and threw in another line, 'And do it imejit'. Unknown to us, a little girl had left her seat in the stalls, walked up the aisle, stood on the other side of the orchestral pit and roared at me, 'Let Cinderella alone, you fat fool.' That to me is what panto is about.

Billa once worked with the great Jack Doyle and Billa invited him to his house. He stayed for lunch. 'He came into our front room, took off his shoes, had a bit of grub and he struck me as a lovely but lonely man. He had appeared in concert at the Country Club Hotel. He sang a few songs and the audience loved him. Later he spoke to me about his loneliness. He had separated from his wife Movita but they had never divorced. He obviously loved her. He was a martyr for the drink.' Jack told Billa that as far back as 1929 he was a millionaire when a million pounds meant something.

Jack Mackesy, the publican, wanted to meet Doyle because there was a dog called Never Say Die and Doyle had won a lot of money on a bet. 'I brought Jack through the English Market on our way to Mackesy's and it took us two hours from the Grand Parade to Oliver Plunket Street. The word had got out that Doyle was heading for town. He had a word for everyone.'

Billa brought other stars to Cork, including Bridie Gallagher and Brendan Grace. Brendan was a late replacement for sports commentator Brendan O'Reilly who had a great ballad voice. Brendan had to do a sports programme for RTÉ, so he sent down 'Bottler' in his place. 'His Grace' went down a bomb on his first visit to a Cork stage.

I suggested to Billa that he had, and continues to have, an amazing life. 'I wouldn't swap it with anybody,' he said. Billa married into a showbiz family, as wife Nell was one half of the Cotter Sisters. Sister Phil and Nell were stars in their own right. One year Phil was Cinderella in Father Mathew Hall and Billa was in panto in the Father O'Leary Hall. The Cotter girls were on the Opera House stage even before Billa would make the place his own.

Billa recalls the years when Chris Sheehan would travel up from Crosshaven to appear with Billa in the pantos. Between the matinee and evening shows, Billa and Chris used to head home to the Lough where the two would dig into a fine feed of bodice, prepared with love by Nell.

Billa's life is less hectic now. His wife, sons, daughters and extended adoring family have him to themselves for Christmas. His beloved Barrs have him on the sideline, on the terrace, in the stand, wherever they play, in whatever grade, as Billa has always sung the 'Blues'.

Theatre's loss was inevitable, but Billa will always have a special place in the hearts of all those who remember how he brightened their lives. The Lough is his stage now, and there he can savour the daily delight of this well-earned and much-deserved, 'walk-on' role.

Chapter 11
Spellbound

Mon Murphy

Monica Murphy has entertained audiences her entire life but as a young girl she thought that she would never get out of the orchestra pit.

Mon's dad, Jerry, was an opera buff. The world famous Carl Rosa Company was in town, so ten-year-old Mon went hand-in-hand with Dad to the old Opera House. The opera was *Faust* and the young girl who was to become one of Cork's own darling comediennes loved the whole sense of magic revealing itself on stage. She wanted to be up there. Life is full of unexplained, seemingly unconnected twists. Mon played the violin, hence her position in the pit, but chance is a fine thing and Mon did get on stage eventually.

Eileen Curran, sister of Chris, was a major artistic force in St Aloysius on the south bank of the Lee. She gave her pupils a marvellous interest in drama and each year there would be a Christmas show at the school. Years before, Eileen was rolling

A tincture of arsenic and some old lace with Mon Murphy and Elaine Stevens
(© private collection)

out younger brother, Chris, in a pram. On the road was a curate in the North Chapel, Father Christy O'Flynn, who was to have a major influence on Cork's artistic life with the founding of the Cork Shakespearean Company in Shandon's shadow. He asked the teenage Eileen if she would like to join the company at the Loft and she did. Later, now a teacher in St Als, Eileen also held private elocution classes that Mon joined. 'Because I played the violin, I'd be down below scraping away and I never got a part on stage while I was in the school.'

Mon, at Inter Cert stage, was invited by Eileen to join the Loft company. Every Sunday morning at 12 noon, Father O'Flynn held centre-stage. 'I was spellbound by the man. He'd tell us stories abut local characters and he'd trace all the relations of the people mentioned. He was madly interested in the welfare of the people. Then he'd suddenly break into something from *King Lear*. He was always rehearsing one play and it'd take months.' When Mon joined they were doing the Scottish play.

> I was hiding in the corner and he turned to me and said that I'd make a good Fleance. I had one line: 'The moon is down I have not heard the clock'; and then, when Banquo is murdered, I had to scream and

run off stage. Fr O'Flynn said to me, 'Mon you went on as if you were apologising for your existence.' But I kept going. We learned more from that man than anyone else.

He'd approach Shakespeare in a deliberate Cork accent. One line in a play was something like: 'Did you pull me by the coat?' Father said it should be, 'C'mere, did you pull me be the coat?' From there the actor advanced to the actual Shakespearean line as written. His approach was always towards proper meaning and interpretation. He gave us a fantastic love of Shakespeare. He gave us confidence. Soon I was to play Ophelia opposite Michael Twomey's Hamlet. Kevin Sheehan was Polonius. He'd never typecast an actor, so I played Puck in *Midsummer Night's Dream*, and then Jessica in *The Merchant of Venice*.

Mon Murphy as Miss Hannigan in full flight as orphanage children dance and shout in a scene from Annie *at the Opera House*
(© private collection)

There was a healthy rivalry between the dramatic nurseries, so if you played with the Loft, it was frowned upon if you also went to James Stack's drama classes in the School of Music. 'Stacky asked me to take a part in the play about Blessed Martin de Porres. It was a tiny part.' Eileen Curran advised Mon that the way to get round it was to tell Fr O'Flynn that the proceeds were going to the Dominican Church on Pope's Quay.

From that time, he never said anything about me performing in a Stacky play. Ignatius Comerford was a very old priest in the play and he was fantastic. Joss Cahill was my husband in the play and he was liable to say anything. We were all around the priest's deathbed and in tears. Ignatius as the priest was to ask, 'Where is Jessica?'; and the answer from Joss was to be, 'She is in the church praying'; but one night he said under his breath, which we heard, but not the audience, 'She's backstage making tea.' Ignatius was heaving with laughter in the bed. Stacky was not happy . . .

I did loads of work for Stacky including *Give Me a Bed of Roses* with Michael McAuliffe, and we did *Holiday Revels* for the whole summer. Chris Whitnell and myself were usually partners. Also on stage were Lorraine Jones, Peg O'Connell, Donal O'Donovan and Sean Riordan, with The McTeggart Dancers. It was a real variety show, the forerunner of *Summer Revels*, directed by Michael Twomey. The comedy, *Give Me a Bed of Roses*, did eight weeks' business.

Stacky began directing musicals and the first one I was in was *The Geisha*, with Finn Scannell, Chris

Sheehan and the lovely Louise Studley. Stacky really looked after his players; he was a very generous man.

Give Me a Bed Of Roses *with Mon Murphy and Michael McAuliffe*
(© private collection)

Mon traces her comedic wellspring back to Father O'Flynn who entertained the impressionable Mon and the rest with his local tales done in the pure Cork accent. 'I'd be hysterical. Then when I'd go to parties, I'd repeat them myself. There was the one about the dumping of the King George monument on the Grand Parade in the river. Another was about a child with the bad bone in the leg, the suggested medical cure in the North Infir, and the reply from the irate mother. There was, too, the song about "The Pride Of Liscarroll", which we sang in Michael McAuliffe's play, *Flynnie.*'

James N. Healy spotted Mon's comic talent and she did a series of roles for him. 'I don't think James was appreciated enough. He was a genius. There were his terrific G and S [Gilbert and Sullivan] shows, his production notes and scores, plus his preparation. He was a broad talent, a fantastic actor. He was an author too – there was his book on castles, [*Castles of County Cork*, Mercier Press, 1988] for which he did all the sketching.'

I wondered what kept Mon going all those years on stage. 'I love to make people laugh. There is a great feedback from comedy. If you do a straight play you will not know until the end if the audience hates you, but in comedy you know after five minutes. I always admired Billa O'Connell for the way he went to win over an audience. He'd come off to the wings and say, "They're tough tonight", but he would not give up until he succeeded in making them laugh.'

Cork Operatic (who had moved to the Father Mathew Hall because the Cork Opera House was unavailable after the fire) planned a production of the great musical *Oklahoma*. There was a problem when the Rev. Guardian of the time read the script and insisted that Ado Annie's big number 'I Can't Say No' be deleted as it was, in his view, too suggestive. The show did go ahead with Mon Murphy singing the song in question but at the Palace, which had retained its theatre licence although it was trading now as a cinema.

It was full circle for Mon when Michael McAuliffe's *Flynnie* and *Flynnie's People* were rip-roaring successes. 'When we were doing them, I could almost hear Father O'Flynn himself. I'd remember him saying, "No, no, you are not getting it at all. That is only the lipstick of the emotion." If Father O'Flynn had not been a priest, he would have been in West End theatre. He could hold his own with the very best. He did appear on stage in Sunday night concerts and he'd bring down the house.'

Mon Murphy is centre of attention with Flynnie's people, Dan Coughlan,
Mairin Prendergast, Kevin Sheehan and Bernie Holland.

Mon considers that some of her finest comedy scripts came
from George Crosbie. 'George wrote loads of stuff for Paddy
Comerford and myself. In the harp sketch, Mon is out in
Brussels flogging poitín. Addressed to the Government of the
day and sung to the air of 'The Spinning Wheel', it ends:

Instead of your guff and financial clangers,
let Ireland get rich, and
let Europe get langers.

Shades, perhaps, of the Lisbon Treaty!

Mon loved the comic roles in the John B. plays. She says, '*The Buds of Ballybunion* was not his best play but Valerie Carroll and myself were two sisters; great parts, they were very funny. We went to the Olympia in Dublin and did very well.'

Mon has never lost her love of getting on stage and is rightly proud of her own one-woman show, *Lunchtime Laughter*, produced by Kenny Lee and directed by Cathal McCabe at the Palace. Kenny saw *Flynnie* and got the idea of a show with Mon going solo. He was determined to get it on stage. Mon mentioned it to her great friend, designer Pat Murray. Typically, Pat said, 'And, why not?' He suggested that Cathal McCabe would direct and Frank Duggan should be at the piano. Mon had been in *Me and My Girl* and *The Halfpenny Bridge*, directed by Cathal. Rehearsal was in Pat's house and it played to great houses in the foyer space at the Everyman Palace.

We have not touched on many performances by Mon, but there is one she will not forget. She loves panto, and always has, but one production of *Aladdin* will stay forever in her memory. She played the genie and she was literally undone by her costume. Doing a big number, with dancers and Aladdin on stage, Mon's top dropped and the audience were in raptures. Mon had no idea that she was uncovered and continued to belt out the number with the dancers frantically trying to point out to her that she was, in fact, topless. One of the Cute Kiddies, in endearing innocence, turned to Eileen Cavanagh in the wings. 'Look Miss, the genie has lost her bubbles.' It was a showstopper but was not repeated.

Another fond panto memory for Mon is working with Gaye Carlile in *Sleeping Beauty*, with Gaye as Fairy Buttercup, Mon as Fairy Dot and Rachael Walsh as Fairy Dimples. Other shows she loves to recall include: the musicals *Oklahoma* and *The*

White Horse Inn, directed by Dan Donovan; the dramatic *Arsenic and Old Lace*, with her great friend, Elaine Stevens, directed by Donn McMullin; *A Country Girl*, the hit musical *Annie*, in which she played Miss Hannigan directed by Larry Oaks. She loved working with directors James Stack, Dan Donovan, Michael McAuliffe, Michael Twomey, Donn McMullin and Catherine Mahon Buckley.

All comedy actors want to play the great dark roles and Mon is not the exception. She particularly loved playing in *Home*, with direction by June McCarthy.

Mon waits in the wings for the next part, the little girl who wanted out of the orchestra pit and has never stopped wondering about that role of a lifetime. She has been the magical, mirth-maker for generations of Cork theatre-goers. Whatever about playing that darkly, dramatic heroine, Mon's gift to her audience is laughter.

Chapter 12
Shock and Awe

Tony Hegarty

The great artistes admit to being nervous before going on stage for a performance. They say also that being funny is a serious business. It is as if performers, the better ones and the more experienced, actually harness that backstage edginess to enhance their performance.

I have watched Tony Hegarty from the wings many times and the warm-up routine is the same, since comedians are creatures of habit. There is the pacing up and down off stage, which seems to be standard practice with the silent mouthing of the lines, and then, on cue, Tony has gone centre-stage straight into his opening patter. If the initial audience reaction is somewhat muted, this could be followed by, 'Are they out there at all?' or, more likely, 'Are ye dead?' Audiences love that chiding and immediately Tony has them on his side. Those are the good nights; but what happens when things do not go to plan and the unforeseen hitch arises?

The multi-faceted, multi-talented Tony Hegarty
(© private collection)

'I have found that I'm at my best when things go wrong. Once, my accompanist's mobile phone rang and it was picked up on his lapel mike. It made a fierce racket and then everything went quiet. I told the audience, "That's the fire brigade. They heard Tony Hegarty was on fire."'

Tony was not always a sure-fire hit and knows what it is like to 'die' on stage, since it is not always possible to park life at the stage door. 'There was a time when I lived with my mother. When she died I could not bring myself to do a show. But I was starving, so I decided to take a gig in Killarney. I was absolutely hopeless on the night. My heart wasn't in it at all. I had to excuse myself right in the middle of the act. No explanation, I just left the room. I could not bring myself to say what was wrong with me. I simply walked off.'

Tony has a particular horror of doing cabaret on certain occasions.

> Seminars? Don't mention seminars to me. Those taking part have been listening to people talking for three days; they're being lectured and there are discussions and then more lectures. For the final evening of the seminar someone has a great idea: why not have an old knees-up – we'll have a dinner and then a cabaret. Problem is that those who were so disciplined for the three days are free at last to sit and chat. The talking starts and understandably does not end when it's time for you to do your act. You're doing your show against a barrage of noise. I hate seminars.

I have always been intrigued by the science of good comedy. How does an artiste unlock laughter in a disparate group of people? Tony would please the US High Command, since his tactic could be loosely described as 'shock and awe'.

> Ever seen two people, two strangers, accidentally bumping into each other in a street and, having apologised, they immediately start laughing? I enjoy shocking people's sensitivity. Also, if you tell a story during an act you will find that there is a certain word that sets up your punch-line.
>
> I enjoy a little vulgarity. I was doing a show one time and I met a priest who had been in the audience.

I felt that I should apologise to him for the content of my show. 'Not at all,' was the reply. 'A little vulgarity is necessary for a healthy mind.'

Who's your man?: Up The Rebels producer Tony Hegarty in the colours talking to his friends
(© Hatchell)

Tony has lifted people's spirits for more than fifty years, but he was not stage-struck as a lad. Hurling and his club, Na Piarsaigh, absorbed him; he gave all his spare time to the northside club which has produced a succession of players wearing the Cork jersey with distinction, including Tony O'Sullivan, the Ó hAilpíns and John Gardiner, to mention just a few.

Now, all these years on, I have the theatre bug and I love to have an audience. I'm not an off-stage comedian. I detest off-stage comedians. My first response to those who ask me to say or do something funny is to say, give me a break. After a hard show all you want is to have a quiet pint, but instead people come up to you to tell you a joke. What I do love is people coming up to me in a store or a street and telling me how much they loved a show that I was in. I glow at that. I take pleasure in it. It is not so much the praise but the fact that you gave a bit of happiness to someone. Others like to talk about the good old days when we had the céilís in the City Hall. They still talk to me about those days and I never tire of listening.

Tony has played with the best in show business. The Nuremore Hotel in Monaghan hosted an all-star cast with the likes of Gay Byrne, Mike Murphy and Dermot O'Brien, and Tony was chosen to represent Cork. Gay loved his Figaro mime act and invited him on the *Late Late Show*. 'Live TV was a big departure for me, but I did it. They were a tough audience. The show itself featured a discussion on the Irish language and emotions were high. There were fireworks. I then came out and did my song about the guards, "I'd Love to Be a Garda". I did a few gags and then Figaro. The place fell apart, that really got them.'

I wondered if Tony's act would travel well outside the country?

> If I got a shilling for every time I was invited to America, I'd be rich. The singer Cathal Dunne, who lives out there, lined up a gig for me. I was to do three shows a night. It was a big cabaret venue and Cathal told me I'd top the Irish comics that were out there. Then at the last minute I opted out, without any regrets.
>
> Accordionist Dermot O'Brien invited me out dozens of times but I did not go. I felt that America would be all brass and tinsel. I thought the audiences, although appreciative, would not get hold of the Corkonian humour.

I pressed Tony on his real reasons for not going Stateside. He admitted, 'It was partly a lack of confidence. It was that kind of insecurity which is in all comics. That same insecurity works to your advantage on stage. There you are standing in the wings waiting to go on and you ask yourself, "How the hell did I come to be here and is there any way out of it?" but you go on.'

Tony toured in the UK with the Regal Showband as a relief act but the highlight for the Cork comedian was a solo appearance in a packed Albert Hall. It was comperèd by Joe Lynch and on the bill were Eileen Donaghy, Brendan Grace and Dermot O'Brien.

> I thought I'd be very nervous but I went out the day before on the *Innisfallen* with Seán Ó Sé. I wrote to and rang all my friends in England. We had the mother and father of a get-together the night before. There were a lot of my friends living in London at that time. I was in a somewhat dazed condition the next day, so I had no nerves on stage. I knew my act so well that I simply stepped out on stage and said I was from Cork. There was a great roar back. It went down a stormer. Joe Lynch said to me after the show that I should come over to England permanently and make my home there. Again I did not, and again, no regrets. I did not want to be famous. When I was young and starting out in show business, I wanted it all, but when I went full-time professional I found that it was a different ball game. When I worked with all the other professionals, I learned that their lives were not their own. I would have found that intolerable.

I toured with Dick Emery and nearly every night there was a row. He was beside himself with nerves before he went on stage. When the show went well he was grand and he'd invite us to his dressing room for a drink. It was pressure, pressure wherever we went. I was the compère.

Handshake and smiles after pre-show tension – MC Tony Hegarty and the late TV star, Dick Emery
(© private collection)

One night in Tralee Tony arrived at the Mount Brandon venue to be asked by Dick where his running order for the show was. There were words exchanged with Tony pointing out that there was no need for one as the show was comprised, in the main, of Dick Emery, followed by another act as Dick did a quick change, then the great man himself again.

It was now running up to curtain time so Tony agreed to act as stage-manager as well as looking after his compère duties. Tony walked across the stage, opening the curtain, and on stage came a beaming Dick. He shook hands with Tony and called for a round of applause for his new-found stage-manager. Proof, surely, that there is no business remotely like show business.

Tony was a much-loved panto performer. He played all the

venues, from the Father Mathew Hall, AOH Hall, Parochial Hall Guarranbraher, to the Opera House; then around the county and over the county bounds. 'I loved pantos, playing to the kids. I'd ad lib like hell when I played the comic roles, though as the Baron you had to stay in character.'

The brothers Tony and Neil provided the laughter in the panto *Red Riding Hood*, presented by the Father Mathew Players in 1952–3. It was scripted by Paddy Kenny, with Agnes O'Sullivan as the Principal Girl, and Principal Boy was Laura Dalton. A version of *Cinderella* at the AOH Hall in 1957 was scripted by Paudie Harris. One critic of the time had this to say about Paudie's ability to make the fairy tale relevant to audiences of the time:

> Topicality is becoming more and more the medium by which the success or failure of a panto is measured. Sketches based on items currently in the news, as well as the cracks of the moment, are the ingredients upon which the successful scriptwriter must base his work, all the while maintaining a balance to ensure that the departures from the theme proper are not overdone. It is in this regard Paudie Harris has scored. Mr Harris is most fortunate in having the assistance of the Hegarty Brothers, Neil and Tony, to fill the parts of the Ugly Sisters. The pair don the garb of mirthmakers with a zest and flair that reaches across the lights to capture the audience from the moment they first appear.

In that show Anne Cooney was Cinders, George O'Mahony was Buttons, Gertie Wine, Prince Charming, and June Moran was Dandini. Charlotte O'Byrne was Fairy Godmother with Con Murphy as Baron Hardup.

There is nothing like a dame: Paddy Coughlan and Tony Hegarty all dressed up and nowhere to go.

In 1956 *Babes in the Wood* had the Neff twins, Carol and Benny, with a very strong line-up of Bill Mahony, Betty McCarthy, Anne Cooney, Tommy Dynes, Tony Hegarty, John McLoughlin, Maureen O'Sullivan, Mary Sweeny, Mary D'Alton and John O'Flaherty. Musical director was Edna McBirney and Eileen Cavanagh's troupe of young dancers stole the show as usual.

In 1957 the *Cork Examiner* could account for five separate productions opening on St Stephen's Day. In that season *Cinderella* at the AOH Hall had a typically strong cast for a Paudie Harris show. It included the wonderful Gertie Wine and the Hegarty Brothers who were the stars of the show.

Tony has always been associated with the northside and his beloved Na Piarsaigh. Before Tony's family crossed the river, they had lived in Evergreen Street and his early schooling was in the South Convent, affectionately known as the South Connie.

The Presentation Sisters, Bernadene and Augustine, must have seen the future, since they cast Tony as the dame, mother of Little Boy Blue, when Tony was 'just about' seven years of age.

Then we moved house to the northside and myself and my brother went to school in the North Monastery. That was September 1939, about two weeks after the Second World War broke out. I remember Neville Chamberlain's 'We are at war with Germany' announcement on the wireless. I was just a boy and had been sitting in the Evergreen soccer club in Crone's Lane.

When I got home I could see my parents were anxious and wondering what was the future for their children with the reality of a World War. When we moved across the city in a horse and cart, it was as if I was moving to a foreign country. That's how it felt to me at the time. My poor mother hated moving. At the time you had a choice of electricity or gas in the new house. My mother had no intention of staying and she did not want to waste money in getting in electricity. She had applied for a transfer back to the southside. When my mother died, at eighty years of age, we still had not got electric light upstairs. She'd only use the gaslights.

My father was from a very old part of Cork,

Curry's Rock, just above Lower John Street. The Hegartys were carriers with floats and side-cars for the 'Yanks' when they'd visit Cork. My mother never did move back across to the southside.

I joined the Cathedral Choir, directed by Aloys Fleishmann. There was a show in the Opera House and he was asked for four lads to sing outside a house in the Micheál MacLiammóir production of *The Man Who Came to Dinner*, with Hilton Edwards in the title role. I sang a little solo and the lads then joined in.

Tony had no idea that he was working with the two greats of the Irish stage at the time, nor was he particularly interested.

My brother Neil was taking a big interest in comedy. He loved to go to the Opera House to see the shows. The Spangle Hill Welfare Guild Hall was built and they were running concerts and we'd go on the Sunday nights. My brother felt that we could do just as well as those on stage. He auditioned and won a competition. When my voice broke and I was no longer a boy soprano, he asked if I would be his feed-man. I didn't fancy it at all although he was mad into it. I was playing hurling with Na Piarsaigh. I remember Sunday evenings, he'd be on his way down Redemption Road to the Opera House and I'd be on the way up. He'd have his stage gear and I'd be carrying my boots, hurley and togs. I'd have to rush home to wash, shave and then run down to the taxis, to join him.

We became very popular. We played every town and village as concerts were all the rage in the late '40s and '50s. We played the Opera House, the Capitol Cinema and the Savoys in Limerick and Cork. Gradually I was getting the show business bug.

Tony Hegarty was born for the business of showbiz. On his own admission a succession of day jobs did not appeal to him at all. 'By day I worked at Egan's jewellers in Patrick Street. I was in the ecclesiastical department. Later I was to train as a watchmaker. Like every other day job, I hated it. I turned down the life of a watchmaker. I did not tell my parents. I then worked in Ford's and Sunbeam Wolsey.' Tony then bursts into song:

We took wool from the flocks and made
full-fashioned socks; you're the pride
of sweet Blackpool, Billy D.

(Billy Dwyer was the respected owner of the Sunbeam Wolsey Company, which provided hundreds of jobs in Blackpool in the northside of Cork City.)

'Another time I joined the Jamaica Banana Company. I was fired when the boss found I had done a matinee and evening show in Bantry when I should be working on the fruit lorry. He suggested that I should stick to show business, which I did. It was 1949.' Years later Tony and the boss met at a Rotary dinner and they laughed at the memory of Tony's move into the world of entertainment.

The Hegarty Brothers topped the bill in such shows as *Hello There*, *Cavalcade* (with Bill Dunlea), *Carnival*, *Tostal Toast*,

Whitsun Revels, Laugh and Be Happy, Curtain Up (with Cecil Sheehan), *Here We Are, Callbox, Merry Omnibus* and *On with the Show.*

I was beginning to have great fun on stage. We got great money at the time. Three guineas was considered very good. Those concerts had terrific line-ups: the brilliant Danny Hobbs, Dick Donegan, Chris Sheehan, Tommy Bridgeman, Donal Kennealy et cetera.

At that time there were separate concert parties or casts, so Cecil Sheehan and his company met before a show at Piggot's music shop in Patrick Street, Tommy Bridgeman's at the Opera House and Danny Hobbs', outside his shop in Patrick Street. He'd close shop and then head off to venues in the county and beyond.

My other passion was hurling with Na Piarsiagh. I played up to intermediate grade. My ambition for Na Pairsaigh, founded in 1943, was that the club would be as good as Glen Rovers. It was a mad ambition of mine and all my efforts went into achieving this. I became chairman and lost ground in show business because of club commitments. I was also manager of the senior team.

Michael Ellard, former Na Piarsaigh star, inter-county hurler, footballer and sports journalist, once described Tony thus: 'He was our manager, trainer, coach, sole selector, medic, psychologist, counsellor and friend.'

Tony went solo when his brother Neil decided to concentrate

on his day job at Whitegate refinery. 'He'd have to get up at six in the morning to catch the seven o'clock car to the refinery for work at 8 a.m. He'd get home for six o'clock and then head down to the Father Mathew Hall for a panto. It was too much.'

Noel Barrett and Pat Sullivan of *Swans* fame told me that, in their view, Neil was the best panto dame of them all. Neil decided to leave show business altogether. He was a terrible loss to the stage.

Tony could not resist the thought of going full-time in showbiz.

I had long decided that I was not cut out for any job other than show business. It snowballed. The cabaret scene developed and I could not handle the bookings. I had my own show. We did Barleycove, Owenahincha, Cobh and Youghal. The line-up included Captain Paddy Kelly, Charlotte O'Byrne, David McInerney, Cathal Dunne, John R. O'Shea and many others.

I'd tell stories, do comedy sketches and mime. I was so busy with the cabaret I was unable to do *Swans* or pantos as often as I would have liked to do so. My first appearance with the *Swans* was out in the Glen Hall in *The Swans of the Glen*, which had been *The Swans of the Lough* when it played on the southside.

In it I played Dinny, which was first played by Bill Mahony. I was Josie Mac too, the role originated by the brilliant Paddy Cotter. I was also a Hare Krishna.

The *Swans* show was typical Cork. 'Give us a lend of the loan of a half pig's head, me mam wants to soften the cabbage.' It was all about cup-of-sugar neighbourliness. Paudie Harris had the Midas touch as a writer. He was a wonderful 'comic situations' man. Dinny and Taigín [Tommy Dynes] were always on the make.

We'd pack the Opera House for three weeks, twice a year, and the critics never stopped knocking it. They did not understand it. It was even suggested that the people of Cork had grown tired of the *Swans*. Not so, as the show sold out again and again.

Bill Mahony directed the *Swans* and one night he answered the critics. He told the audience that the *Swans* had been constantly criticised, but that there was an old saying that criticism, like medicine, should be dispensed only by those who knew how.

The success of the *Swans* lay in the fact that there was a great script delivered by great comedians. Der Donovan and Charlotte O'Byrne were hilarious as the country folk. Here is the powerful cast list for *The Swans Fleadh Cheoil,* staged at the Opera House in April 1978: Paddy Cotter (Josie), Tommy Dynes (Taigín), Paddy Coughlan (Dolly), Tony Hegarty (Dinny), Pat Sullivan (Cadger), Noel Barrett (Bowler), Charlotte O'Byrne (Roisín), Pat Harris (Rory), Christy Morris (Mike), Maurice O'Donovan (The Yank), Mai Murphy (Maeve), Donie Gleeson (ESB Ganger), Patrick Cotter (Liam) and Finbarr Cotter (Jer).

'One evening Danny La Rue came backstage after a show and wanted the company to tour to London. He thought it a marvellous evening of comedy. This was when Danny himself was at the height of his powers. The company said at the time that we would go to London, but later decided that the Cork dialect might not travel well and we never did go to London as a company.'

There is a showbiz story that one evening one of the *Swans* cast was injured and rushed to the Mercy Hospital. The doctor, who was from foreign parts, was told by the injured party that he was a Swan. The doctor felt that the patient might be concussed. He told other members of the cast who had gone to the hospital that one of their own thought that he was a Swan. They reassured the perplexed doctor that they were Swans too!

In 1980 Paudie Harris chose some of his best material and *The Best of the Swans* opened at the Opera House, to huge acclaim. The cast featured: Der O'Donovan, Charlotte O'Byrne, Christy Morris, Bill Mahony, Tommy Dynes, Tony Hegarty, Paddy Coughlan, Noel Barrett, Pat Sullivan, Pat Quirke, Moira Power, Donie Gleeson and Liam Harris, plus the boys and girls of the Lough Community and Variety Club. Bill Mahony directed, with design by Pat Murray and musical direction by Ronnie O'Shaughnessy.

In 1981 it was *The Swans Go Disco*, with another powerful line-up and featuring Marie Twomey. There was a final revival of the *Swans* in the 1990s at the Everyman Palace. The *Swans* shows were really *the* success story down all those decades when Cork audiences were enraptured by a world of comedy that captured the collective heart and soul of its citizens.

Tony Hegarty appeared in some memorable pantos under the direction of Michael Twomey in the Opera House and at the Everyman Palace. In 1996 he teamed up with another great Cork showman, Paddy Comerford, for an excellent production of Lionel Bart's *Oliver!*, staged by Fermoy Choral Society, with Valerie Carroll as Nancy.

Tony has truly been a man for all showbiz seasons since that first night in *Little Boy Blue* in South Convent. There were his bill-topping years with brother Neil, then as a solo performer from Opera House to Albert Hall, London. There were his years as Master of Ceremonies and impresario when the showbands (the Freshmen in particular) were in full swing; the concert and cabaret nights; and there were the packed City Hall ceilís, with Jimmy Shand, Dermot O'Brien, the Galloglass, Donal Ring, the Alexander Brothers, the Bon Accords, Kenneth McKellar, Andy Stewart and Maisie McDaniel.

Tony produced a Cavalier company version of *A Streetcar Named Desire*, with Rachael Murphy (of *Fair City*), Conor Dwane (of Skylight Theatre Company) and Elmarie Mawe (of *Art House*, 96FM), with direction by Michael McAuliffe. He also appeared in Michael's play, *Rag Tales*, and was particularly funny in Michael Twomey's production of John B. Keane's *Matchmake Me Do*, adapted by Terry Byrne.

Two productions that brought me into personal contact with Tony were the revival of G. P. Gallivan's *The Stepping Stone* in 1997, and my own revue-style history of Cork GAA, *Up the Rebels*. Tony produced both plays with the infectious enthusiasm and good humour that are his hallmarks, adding his own extensive knowledge of the GAA to make *Rebels* a resounding success.

The Stepping Stone was directed by Neil Pearson. It starred Michael Murphy as Collins and Rebecca Allman as Kitty Kiernan, with Dick Healy reprising his role as Arthur Griffith, a link with the orginal production in 1963, when Dan Donovan directed and Michael McAuliffe was Collins.

Laughter surrounds, permeates and uplifts all those who are fortunate to fall into Tony's company. What other comedian could walk onto a stage and immediately begin to enquire after the health of an audience and the odds on their imminent passage into the next world – and have them howling with delight? He's intrinsically a Cork comedian who can literally hurtle from burlesque, to operatic mime, to pantomime and finally to farce; he's a performer, promoter and producer. They broke the mould after they fashioned Tony Hegarty.

Chapter 13
The Quality Mark

David McInerney

Much play is made about the incredible talent treading the boards of Cork theatres in the second half of the last century, but the reality was that this was not a cast of thousands, but rather a relatively small group of remarkably versatile and skilled performers who moved smoothly from one discipline to another without any apparent diminution of quality.

A splendid example of this versatility was David McInerney. David has always been blessed with a truly magnificent coffee-brown baritone voice of splendid timbre and an attractive stage presence. He was a star at a time when the Cork Operatic Society, the Nigel Hay Productions Gilbert and Sullivan group, and the Collins Musical Society produced a succession of shows from the popular repertoire, including the Savoy Operas and many much-loved musical comedies.

Educated at the Christian Brothers on Sullivan's Quay, David played the violin, but it was his voice that attracted the attention in the North Cathedral Choir. Members then included Leo White, who became Registrar at University College, Cork (UCC), Paddy Murphy, a butcher from Oliver Plunkett Street, and Jim Stack.

David McInerney in full regalia for his role as The Mikado *in 1976*

'I had joined the Cork Harbour Board in 1948. I was in the engineering and maintenance department for six years before joining finance, where I remained until retirement in 1989. I sang in my first concert around '52 or '53, but within a year I found myself in my first opera, *La Traviata*, at the old Opera House for the Cork Grand Opera Group. Funnily enough, I had only a small role but, to my surprise, I got a commendation from the *Examiner* critic of the time.' A programme note makes interesting reading now: 'In consideration for the artistes, patrons are requested to please refrain from smoking in the theatre.' Changed times indeed.

In *La Traviata*, David was the Marquis D'Obigny and the cast included guest and local performers: Patricia Baird, Joan Booth, Bruce Dargavel, Brycham Powell, William Deasy, Tadgh O'Laohaire, Bob Carlile, Maura Hayes, Jim Crockett and Jim Ryan. Later he appeared in *Rigoletto* with William Dickie in the title role. The programme also noted some coming attractions at the old theatre that year – namely Jimmy

O'Dea in *Spice of Life*, followed by Wallas Eaton in *Seagulls Over Sorrento*.

In October 1954, David joined the cast for a concert at the Opera House which included Dick Donegan, Albert Healy, Maura Hayes and Betty Isaac. Also appearing that night was Paddy Cotter, one of the finest in a Cork's long list of great panto dames. A famous visitor to the Opera House that year was the great Sadler's Wells singer Marian Studholme in *Lucia di Lammermoor*. In November 1955 there were productions of *Aida* and *Barber of Seville*, with David as the servant Fiorella.

Who could have known that the beautiful old theatre would be destroyed the following month by that disastrous fire? There was a move to the Palace, but the loss of the larger capacity available at the Opera House put further strain on companies who were trying to attract top singers from overseas, to be supported by home-grown talent. Opera, light or grand, has always been under financial pressure and it is remarkable that Cork companies – particularly the Cork Operatic Society, James N. Healy's Nigel Hay Productions and Collins Musical Society – managed to stay afloat and provide such remarkably high-quality entertainment for thousands during this difficult time.

I believe that a production of Gilbert and Sullivan's *Utopia Limited*, staged in the Father Mathew Hall in 1958, has not been repeated in Cork – and it is worthy of recall. It caused quite a stir; the cast was very much a 'who's who' of stage entertainment in the city at the time. James N. Healy was the King and David McInerney was Goldbury, the visiting business guru. The cast included: Norman Butler, Dan Coughlan, Pierre Blanc, Gerry Rearden, John de Foubert, Fred South, Cyril Neville, Gordon Blair, Michael Herley, Mary Cullinane,

Roberta Fitzgibbon, Siobhán O'Brien, Ronnie O'Shaughnessy, Flora Kerrigan, Dom O'Callaghan, Mary Heffernan and Barry Hassett.

The debonaire David McInerney in a scene from a production of Gilbert and Sullivan's Utopia *at the Father Mathew Hall in 1958*

(© G. and V. Healy)

Maura Hayes, originally a pupil with John Horne, was at this point tutoring David and delighted, no doubt, in his rapid progress. David recalls:

I wanted to learn singing with the stage in mind. I also wanted to learn stagecraft and there was the bonus that Jim Stack was in the original group, which came out of the Cathedral Choir. I went to Stack's class in the School of Music where I met Michael McAuliffe, Donal O'Donovan, Brendan Fehily, Maura Murphy, Vass Anderson and they were all getting into the art of theatre.

Stack had an interesting way of working with you as his student. He gave you a small piece to do and he'd ask you to work on that for the next class or the one after. Then you went into class and did it. He'd criticise it or ask others their opinion and at the end of the year he'd put on a play, and if he figured you were worthy of a part, you got it. It was 1960 and James N. wanted me to be Danilo in *Merry Widow* at the Palace Theatre and James Stack wanted me to be Hamlet's uncle, King Claudius.

David was feeling, for the first time, the pressure of being in demand for what could be described as roles at either end of the performance spectrum. There was a compromise and David played the lesser role of the Ghost in *Hamlet* and Danilo in *The Merry Widow*. The latter was a role he was to make his own and reprise many times in his stage career. Remarkably Danilo is a role for a tenor, and David was a baritone. There was a way to get around the problem.

James N. brought me up to his house on Grattan Hill and he played a record of the Austrian Eric Kunz. He was also a baritone and he avoided high tenor by speaking some of the phrases, which was also done to great effect when Rex Harrison played Professor Higgins in *My Fair Lady*. Yet another way was found. The musical arrangements for *Merry Widow* and other operettas were now given to amateur groups. They were transposed, brought down in pitch and rescripted, so now Danilo could be a baritone. I rehearsed and rehearsed and then it was announced that a famous English soprano was to come over and sing the title role. Joyce Blackham had been understudy to the great artiste June Bronhill from Australia. The problem was that Ms Blackham wanted to do the role as originally penned.

Here I was doing my first big part and there is this problem. However, it all worked out as we did not really sing together 'til near the end of the operetta.

Danilo established David, and his playing opposite such as star as Ms Blackham went down a treat with the packed houses.

That role of Danilo [in 1960] was the first time I was conscious of comedy in a stage role. Danilo is a devil-may-care sort of guy. James N. was the Ambassador and Danilo is his aide who has no interest in the job, but just wants to be in Maxim's with the girls. It is a lovely script.

James N. directed us. He was a very thorough director; everything was worked out. I was lucky to see some of his preparatory notes and he had everything sorted in advance. We were very lucky that the manager at the Palace, Der Breen, was so interested in theatre from his Theatre Guild days in Presentation College.

David's rapid progress on stage created its own problems:

From that *Merry Widow* I was in demand as a lead singer and that caused the problem of finding the time to rehearse and play the different roles. Also the Palace was primarily a cinema, so the block-time for theatre was small and everybody was looking for the same slots.

That *Merry Widow* was just one of those things that took off. Joyce and I clicked on stage and all the support performances were very good. We began with a gala performance. There was terrific atmosphere about the whole fortnight. We were even applauded when we appeared on stage. Joyce Blackham was the talk of the town. She was demanding about her work but we got on great.

There is a lovely story about David's performance opposite the very beautiful Joyce. When a Cork wit saw their fond embrace at the point where the Widow and Danilo swear their love for each other at last, David is pressed to Joyce's bosom and the remark was heard, 'That's the finest pair of earmuffs I ever saw anyone wearing.' David had encountered comedy on the panto stage as far back as 1958 when he appeared in a Paudie Harris-scripted panto, *Robinson Crusoe*. Directed by Bill Mahony, it had the line-up that would go on to produce one of the most successful series of shows ever to hit an Irish stage, the *Swans*.

Robinson Crusoe was played by Mary Cronin, Captain Kitty by Billa, and the cast also included Olive Cullen, Paddy Coughlan, David McInerney, Der Donovan, Charlotte O'Byrne, Finn Scannell, Paudie Atkinson, and Jim Noonan.

Back to the musical stage, and David was once again faced with a performance dilemma. He was cast as the Student Prince. David felt that the role of Danilo was a reflection of his own personality, but that this was not the case with Romberg's Student Prince. 'You could not have found a bigger change of character. I had no problem with Danilo, but I did ask myself, "Can I really do this?"'

David's concerns were allayed when his performance was critically acclaimed by the *Cork Examiner*. 'Once again his striking stage presence was one of his chief attributes and the sincerity of his acting was very evident. The role fitted him to perfection and he got the most out of it.'

When Jimmy Bellchamber came over from England to direct *My Fair Lady*, he had got from the Cork Operatic a list of the cast and who was playing each role. When I was introduced to him, he never again forgot my name. I was a total stranger but he treated the entire cast in the same way. He was an extremely good producer.

I did most of my comedy roles directed by James Stack. In 1960 it was *Not in the Book*. Director Stack had this to say about David's performance: 'You gave the part just the right touch of sympathy and tolerance. A most likeable Police Inspector. Excellent!'

Utopia with the G and S group, gave me my first big part and I received good notices. It was a very clever show about this island in the South Pacific to where experts from other parts of the world were brought and I was the Financial Expert. I did *Iolanthe* in the Palace, but as the G and S repertoire was now

The versatile David McInerney in Garda Sergeant mode.

running out James N. turned his attention to the operettas and it was the best thing he ever did. Without that decision by Jim Healy I would not have sung in *Merry Widow*, *La Belle Hélène* and the other great shows. I was still learning.

So the singer who was in so much demand was anxious to do straight roles, since it was less taxing vocally and a change from the musicals and operettas.

> I was President of the Institute of Personnel Management and we had our annual conference. They were looking for entertainment and I decided to get Cha and Miah for them. On the way to Dublin myself and Michael Twomey were talking about shows and the concept of the revue-type show. It fitted in with James N.'s suggestion for a show much like the *Tops of the Town* shows as part of the Theatre of the South summer season at the new Opera House; and *Summer Revels* was born, directed by Michael and with my own participation.

David recalls that the *Tops* shows were something of a nightmare. The national quarter-finals were held in the Opera House in Cork and he was MC. 'One side of the house would be falling around the place with laughter, as they were supporting that show. The other half of the house was in stony silence. Then when it was coming up to results time, stage-manager Tommy Cuthbert would be shouting to me behind the half curtain to keep things going, as they were not ready, so

I'd sing a song and tell a few stories. I never liked one-liners, so I'd always tell a funny story.'

All that plus the *Swans*, then the *Revels* – and then there were also the Barleycove Hotel evenings in west Cork for Barra Ó Tuama. Those shows featured Seán Ó Sé, John R. O'Shea, Christy Morris, Jack Murphy, Olive Cullen, Teresa Griffin, Anne Brennan, Frank Duggan and many other guest performers.

> The *Swans* were phenomenal. I began with them over in the CCYMS when they did more of a variety show than the scripted shows, which really made them famous. I'd sing with Mary Cronin. There'd be a scene and we'd fit the duet to suit that. I can remember doing an excerpt from Schubert's 'Lilac Time'.
>
> Bill Mahony, as director and actor, was the linchpin of that group. They then went to the Opera House and I appeared in most of their shows. Primarily I was a singer but I'd be drafted in as a garda. There were two other comic parts that came my way. The first was more caricature, as I was a loony Professor in UCC. I played it to the hilt. I was also an Arab sheik. It was the time of the oil crisis in the '70s. The head of OPEC was a handsome Arab called Sheik Yemani. I was cast as Sheik O'Mahony, or, as Tommy Dynes used to call me during the show, Shaky Mahony.
>
> My admiration for the Swans was immense, as they were such a talented group of people. In many respects, in my view, they were under-rated. They had

the greatest rapport between stage and audience that you could possibly imagine. They were in touch with the 'common man'. Billa O'Connell had the same capacity. There was always a story and the more unlikely the story, the zanier it was for the audience.

It would take a book, which I hope he might consider writing some day, to reflect the sheer volume of stage work done by David over those decades. At the same time he was always meticulous in his onerous day job with the Harbour Board. But there was a price to be paid for such effort. David's health suffered.

As David recalls, backstage at the Opera House one evening Tommy Cuthbert said to David after a show:

'Old stock, you are spending too much time here.' I became ill and lost stones in weight. After a stay in hospital, I met the matron and she said me: 'You are grand now, but would you do me one favour? Would you ever look at your birth certificate now and again?' That was very good advice.

I was never conscious of stage fright. As long as I knew what I was doing, I was not conscious of any stress. I can look back now and realise that though I did not suffer from post-show stress as others did, in all that time I never had a replacement. There was no stand-in so, if I could not do a show, there was simply no show. Looking back now that was the worst pressure of all.

My average year was that I'd start with the panto, which was followed by a spring show, probably with

G and S. Then there was a *Swans* show and getting
down to Barleycove every other weekend. I'd do
concert evenings at Blackrock Castle during the
summer. Then I'd have the rehearsals and
performances for *Summer Revels*, involving duets with
Marie Twomey and parts in various sketches. I'd
compère *Tops of the Town* on Sunday nights. I'd begin
preparing for another operetta in the autumn and
then rehearsals for another panto season.

At random, I decided to research one year (1960) in the life of
David McInerney, singer, host, actor, and comedian. It reads
like this:

- *Cinderella* at the Father Mathew Hall, direction by James N.
  Healy, with musical direction by Bernard Geary and a cast
  which included: Roberta Fitzgibbon, Charlie Kelleher, Ann
  Brennan, Liam O'Connell, Paddy Coughlan, Leonora
  McCarthy, Bill Coughlan, Siobhán O'Brien and Ronnie
  O'Shaughnessy. David was the King that year.
- Artane Boys Band concert in March.
- *The Merry Widow* with the Gilbert and Sullivan Group.
  Some of the *Widow* stars, including David, then toured to
  Waterford, Clonmel and Macroom.
- David was the Inspector in James Stack's *Not in the Book* and
  he was on the bill of *Gilbert and Sullivan Memories*, to mark
  the opening of the Group Theatre in South Main Street on
  27 October 1960.
- Concert in the Capitol Cinema where David appeared with
  Billa and Frank Kelleher.
- He somehow found time to take part in the *Lively Is The Lee*

show at Radio Éireann studios and then went into rehearsals for the thirty-seventh panto at the Father Mathew Hall, *Old King Cole*.

Ten years on, had David's career slowed down at all? Research results proved otherwise:

- *Aladdin* at the Opera House, with Paddy Cotter and Der Donovan.
- The reprise of the 1960s staging of *The Merry Widow*, with Joyce Blackham in the title role and David again as Danilo. Produced by Nigel Hay in the Opera House, the show experienced a pre-opening night drama when Joyce fell ill on the opening day. James N. called on her understudy, Marie Twomey, to take over the role at a few hours' notice, which she did to acclaim. Joyce was able to take over again a few nights later, but Marie played the matinees.
- A brilliant Cork stage première of *My Fair Lady* by the Cork Operatic Society, with Kevin Sheehan as Higgins, Angela Jenkins as Eliza and David her father, Alfred P. Doolittle. This was a production that is remembered so well by many musical comedy lovers. For David the standout performance came from Kevin Sheehan as Henry Higgins. 'Kevin was a fine actor who, because of his job, was not able to avail of the roles for which he would have been ideally suited. I could not have made a finer comparison [than] between Rex Harrison and Kevin Sheehan. Kevin was that good. I would not pick one above the other. Kevin was really outstanding in a wonderful cast.'
- There followed two musicals in succession and then some drama: Joseph Tomelty's *Is the Priest at Home?*, directed by

Bill Mahony, with David as Father Malin in a strong cast, including: Denis Harrington, Michael Riordan, Ronnie O'Shaughnessy, Noel Murphy, Pat Sullivan, Maeve Delaney, Chris Sheehan, Mary Foley and Tony Duggan.

- In October there was another *Merry Widow*, with David's Danilo opposite Mary O'Callaghan's Widow at the Saint Francis Xavier Hall in Dublin.
- That same month, David was in *The Swans Join Up*.

From 1985, David was stage front again with his informed and informal hosting of the hugely popular Barra Ó Tuama operatic gala series in Cork City Hall, the Dublin Concert Hall, and many other city venues, including Cardiff and London. Barra was meeting a demand for evenings of great arias, duets and trios performed by world class artistes with fine accompanists and often orchestras.

David entertained for five decades. Top singing star, versatile actor, in straight or comic roles, David McInerney left his mark on the word of entertainment in its broadest sense.

Town and gown: Professors of Codology – Der Donovan and Dave McInerney

Chapter 14
The Flying *Swans*

The Essence of Cork

The success story of the *Swans* is worth a book in itself. Any attempt to recapture those times when the *Swans* were literally flying high would be, at best, an inadequate recall of what was a showbiz phenomenon. Sadly, the 'senior citizens'of Bridewell Lane – Josie, Taigín, Dolly and Dinny – are no longer with us; the genius who created them, Paudie Harris, has also passed to his eternal reward.

We must make do now with a recall of their exploits, when they made the theatres of Cork reverberate with uncontrollable laughter and whether we cared to admit it at the time, we saw a little (or a lot) of ourselves in those characters. Or, at the very least, we knew someone who resembled one of the characters up there on stage.

Searching for the secret of the Swans' success is, in a sense, a futile exercise; they were loved by their legions of fans over decades. If you have to analyse something that was as naturally

Cork as drisheen and crubeens, then you may miss the essential ingredient of all great comedy, spontaneity.

Thankfully some of those personalities are still very much with us; the people who shared the stage with the 'McCarthys' and the 'O'Sullivans' and packed houses for weeks on end, buttressing box office figures, keeping theatres open, much as popular pantos do to this day.

A flock of Swans including Noel Barrett, Maurice O'Donovan, Christy Morris, Colette Good, Tommy Dynes, Pat Sullivan, Paddy Cotter and Der Donovan with the Cavanagh Dancers

I came across a *Swans of the Lee* programme for the Father Mathew Hall in 1960. Interestingly the O'Sullivans had not yet arrived in Bridewell Lane, since they were then the Fitzgerald family, comprised of Dolly (Billa O'Connell), Dinny (Bill Mahony) and their son Liam (Bob Carlile Jnr). The McCarthys were already in full flight, with Paddy Cotter as

Josie, Der Donovan as Taigín, and Ann O'Brien as daughter Katy. Bob Carlile Snr was Terry O'Malley, the garda was Donie Kenneally and the two Corporation employees were Charlie Kelleher and Eddie Mullins.

There are those who still remember what it was like to sit in a crowded dressing room with the likes of director and actor Bill Mahony, Paddy Cotter, Tommy Dynes and Paddy Coughlan as they readied for another show.

'The situation is this' – Pat Sullivan and Tommy Dynes can't see the woods from the trees.

While researching this book, I met one of Paudie's sons, Liam, who is deputy stage-manager in the Opera House. The image of the writer locked away in a quiet room writing furiously is not his memory of his famous dad. Liam recalls that Paudie always wrote in the room with the TV on loud and clear. Paudie felt no sense of distraction.

Liam is the proud possessor of his dad's very first script, typed on his trusty Royal typewriter. Liam remembers going to the Opera House as a youngster and listening to the great Noel Purcell talk about theatre. He recalls the night Danny La Rue was in the audience for a *Swans* show in the Opera House and the suggestion was made that he would sing 'On Mother Kelly's Doorstep' at the end of the show. But on that occasion one of Cork's most famous exiles did not go on stage.

Liam believes that it was affection for Dinny and Taigín (as played by Bill Mahony and Tommy Dynes) that prompted the placing of Oisin Kelly's two remarkably 'Swan-like' figures outside the County Hall when they were moved from their position in the Crawford Gallery where they had been on exhibition. The I.T.G.U.N. had first commissioned them for Liberty Hall in Dublin and when planning permission was refused by Dublin City Council, the figures were subsequently donated to the council and were sited in front of the County Hall in 1976.

Paudie Harris, the creator of the Swans, a showbiz phenomenon in Cork

Now a third generation Harris, Liam's son Patrick, has joined his dad in the Opera House as part-time usher. Liam, his brother Pat, and sister Siobhán, have all appeared in *Swan* shows.

In the mid-1960s writer Paudie introduced the great Cadger and Bowler to the fans. Corporation workers extraordinaire, Cadger (Pat O'Sullivan) was the ganger who had turned the art of delegation into a fine art, while Bowler (Noel Barrett) was his 'buttie', who got things done with varying degrees of success.

In 2008, almost sixty years after they appeared as the Ugly Sisters (Pentacitis and Tonsilitis) in a Paddy Noonan touring panto, Pat and Noel appeared as Cadger and Bowler in the hit charity series, *Cork on Show*, in the Opera House. They went down a bomb, confirming that good comedy does not have a sell-by date.

In talking to Pat and Noel, I got some idea of just how much they still love getting on stage and making people laugh. Remarkably, they claim never to have fallen out or even to have had a cross word with each other – this in a business where egos can easily lead to bust-ups, even on stage during a performance.

When we were young: Noel Barrett (second from right, front row) with his companions in Taibse

All these years on, they are now able to pick and choose their shows, preferring to do the charity gigs where they feel they are giving something back to a business that has been a major portion of their lives since they were schoolboys. (For Noel schooldays were spent at Greenmount, and for Pat, at Sullivan's Quay.)

Pat has retired from Córas Iompair Éireann (CIÉ). A Barrs man through and through, he figured prominently on senior county winning teams, sporting the blue jersey. On leaving school, Noel worked with Pope's Garage and then ran his own motor factor business until he 'retired to his hobby', making model airplanes. He has 'flown' for Ireland all over the world. He has also constructed detailed models in molecular form for a major drug company and he has built scale models of factories and stadia around the country.

I was left in no doubt, however, that their appearances in the *Swans*, pantos, and later, *Summer Revels*, gave them the greatest satisfaction of all. Noel recalls:

> *Swans* brought Cork to life on stage. You could identify with any of the characters that Paudie Harris created. There are Cadgers and Bowlers everywhere. In those days, walk down Castle Street, into Cornmarket, and you'd meet a Dolly and a Josie. If you called to the old Labour Exchange on George's Quay, you'd encounter a Dinny or Taigín.
>
> When Paudie Harris wrote something, it was always possible that it could happen. It was unlikely, but it was plausible and believable. Any scene he came up with, you never felt that it could not happen. He grappled with the problem of bringing our characters, Cadger and Bowler, into the lane for each show. Three months before one show, he called to my shop and said that he had worked out their entry. He has seen a ganger pointing to weeds and he was followed by his pal, spraying them as they went along. The next show Cadger arrived on stage

pointing out to Bowler the weeds on the quay-wall. Poor Dolly had a plant outside the door. Josie asks, 'What kind plant is it?' 'Dat's Dinny's prize "Roady-dan-drum",' Dolly tells her. Cadger points to it and Bowler sprays it – the plant wilts. All hell breaks loose. It was all done by that magical man backstage, Tommy Burke. He had tied up the plant with gut and let it loose as the spray hit it.

Another time Paudie has us coming over a quay wall in a frogman's outfit having checked the drains in the river. Dolly and Josie thought the lads were from outer space. More mayhem.

In another scene the lads from City Hall are attempting to unblock the unmentionable in Dolly's toilet, stage right. After much huffing and puffing, the extended brush erupts in the house opposite, stage left, driving Taigín to centre stage, in a state of undress. He tells Josie that he has been attacked by a hedgehog. Madness but totally effective, and how the audience loved it.

Another scene that brought the house down was set in a crypt, not the most likely place for laughs but the *Swans* team managed it and, it is recalled by *Swans* fans to this day.

Noel and Pat feel that the success of the *Swans* was due to the creative forces at play with Paudie's scripting, good direction by Bill Mahony, and performers comfortable and natural at what they were doing on stage. Noel explains:

> One of the secrets of the *Swans* was that we played it dead seriously and in character, which made it all the funnier for the audience. Director Bill Mahony often

left it up to yourself as to how to play a particular scene. During rehearsals Paudie would stop you and say, 'That's not a Cadger line, give that to Bowler.'

Bowler was saucy, whereas Cadger was a very serious guy, very religious, who regularly stated that he was a sodality man and was a member of the Third Order. Paudie allowed for your ad libs, which came out in rehearsals. They were a panic, mainly held above in Greenmount School, the College on the hill, as it was known. Three of us had gone to school there, myself, Paddy Cotter and Paddy Coughlan.

Christy Morris, Maurice O'Donovan, Pat Sullivan, and Noel Barrett in a typical Swans scene

Rehearsal for the *Swans* were, to say the least, interesting. The action may have been unusually complicated but it was rehearsed for the first time on the Friday and they opened without a hitch on the following Monday. One scene involved a ladder on wheels and had the catchphrase, 'Come out now'. Noel has painful memories of this, as he fell from the ladder and cracked some ribs. The show ran for another five weeks and Noel completed the run in some pain but in the best tradition of showbiz.

Pictured from left: Pat Sullivan, Paddy Cotter, Tommy Dynes. Bill Mahony, Paddy Coughlan and Noel Barrett.

Paddy Cotter played Josie perfectly as a very innocent, naive woman. She asks Dolly how to cook sausages and is told to clean them just like fish and then cook them. When asked afterwards how she got on with the sausages, she comments, 'Very disappointing, sure there was nothing left to eat when I cleaned them out.' It was very basic humour but, when delivered in character, it invariably worked. Noel says:

Paddy was a very generous actor to play with on stage. If you came up with an ad lib, he would do everything to build it up for the next night. He'd never upstage you. We did concerts and pantos with him and he was a brilliant ad libber himself. He was one of the very best.

Paddy Coughlan in contrast played Dolly as a brazen woman. Dolly lost her temper very easily and Paddy never stepped out of character. He was a great team player and Paudie wrote his lines so that Dolly could deliver those caustic remarks.

Bill Mahony was an excellent director. Once he had the script, he'd mould it and it would work. He was brilliant when Dinny had one too many. He was so convincing on stage. As a director for the type of stuff we did, he was great. He'd suggest ways of delivering lines. He'd listen to his actors.

Tommy Dynes was Taigín who hated the idea of work in any shape or form. Tommy played a quiet character with wonderful facial expression and use of hands. He'd come out with lines from Paudie Harris, which would be so unexpected from his character. He said in one sketch that he'd fancy a 'Matchies Raaza'. Dinny would say, 'No, no Taigín, you means, Mateuse Jose'.

Noel and Pat reminded me of one of the great scenes from *Swans* when Taigín was taken off the dole, much to his annoyance, and given a night-watchman's job, complete with hut and coal brazier. Taigín would take the few steps from his house to the hut, with Dolly crying at his going on such a journey, saying she was going to miss him 'terrible', even though he was only a few feet away from his doorstep in the middle of Bridewell Lane.

Wheeler dealers – Pat Sullivan, Bill Mahony, Tom Cotter, Noel Barrett

Stage lights down, there was only the glow of lighting coal. Minutes later Dolly was out for 'the lend of a loan of a few lumps of coal for the fire'. Then Josie arrives to fry a sausage on the open fire. Cadger and Bowler pass by pushing a piano. Before long there is a full-blown singsong in the street, with Paddy Coughlan, an accomplished pianist, leading the way and Taigín, surrounded by his friends and neighbours, no longer on his lonely vigil in the Lane.

Certainly *Swans* was a godsend for the new Opera House, which opened its doors in 1965. Bill Twomey was then manager and could see that the *Swans* were ideal for the big stage and certain to improve the revenue position of the theatre. It had been built by the citizens and people wanted to see the *Swans* play it, since they had been loved by the city since their start in the early 1950s, when they played Father O'Leary Hall, Father Mathew Hall and Glen Hall.

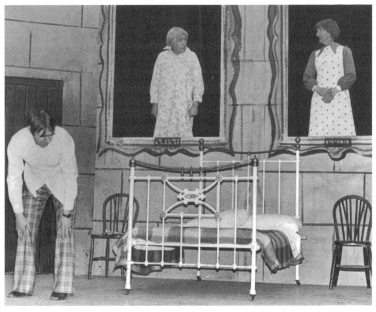

Framed: Paddy Cotter and Paddy Coughlan wonder what Noel Barrett is getting up to in a scene from The Swans.

The Opera House had planned to stage the comedy *Boeing, Boeing* with Joe Lynch, but instead opted for *The Swans of the Lee* for the traditional final two weeks of Lent (mission time in city churches), running up to the Monday, Tuesday and Wednesday of Holy Week, with closure for the Easter ceremonies. The *Swans of the Lee* was so successful that it was brought back after Easter for another two weeks. Noel remembers one particular scene in Cadger and Bowler's first ever appearance in the Opera House.

'It was twilight. They simply leant on their brushes, frozen in the moment, as the Montforts sang 'In a Summer Place'. Anytime since that I hear that song, I feel very emotional, as I remember our first time on that stage.'

Pat and Noel consider that Paudie Harris did a great job in creating all the characters in *Swans*, managing to convince members of the theatre-going public that they were 'real life'. Many even believed that Josie and Dolly were real women, not men pretending to be women in women's clothes.

Art imitated real life once again, on the occasion when a promoter of a celebrity concert actually went to the City Hall to book Cadger and Bowler for his show. He was convinced that they really were working there. The most loved 'Corporation workers' ever to grace a stage confused another gentleman, too. Convinced that they truly worked for the Corporation, a member of the public enquired if they might help him sort out a particular planning problem, which involved the building of an additional bathroom in his house. Cadger and Bowler, theatre's 'Mr Fixits', were unable to oblige. It was simply that the characters in the *Swans* had hidden depths and were founded on real life.

As other characters developed over the years, they were played by Der Donovan, Maurice O'Donovan, David McInerney, Christy Morris, Charlotte O'Byrne, Mary Foley, Siobhán O'Brien and so many others. They were all part of an extended community that lived down Bridewell Lane, where the pace was slower and life was more fun.

Life with the *Swans* would be fame enough for most performers, but director Michael Twomey knew that Cadger and Bowler would fit perfectly into his all-star line-up for *Summer Revels* in the 1970s. They were a major attraction in that incredible cast and for the people who enjoyed the show, it was no doubt great to catch up with the city's most famous workers.

Once, just once, Cadger and Bowler were caught out on stage. In 2007 they agreed, at the request of the *Cork on Show* co-organiser, Kevin Sanquest, to do a topical sketch about the clamping of cars, with the two lads as the dreaded clampers. It was suggested that they might work the sketch in such a way that the then Lord Mayor, Councillor Michael Aherne, could be written into it. What they did not know was that Manus O'Callaghan, organiser of Cork Person of the Year, was waiting in the wings to surprise the two comedians with their very own monthly award, which marked their huge contribution to Cork comic theatre over an incredible fifty-six years.

During the 1940s and 1950s, there may have been poverty in Cork, but there was a 'richness' to life – people may have lived in each other's pockets, but they would never see a neighbour in want if they had something to give in support. I once wrote, 'Lanes are little streets that never wanted to grow up. Happy in their reach-out-and-touch intimacy . . . Many are long since gone dark . . . their former presence marked, brassily, on pavements for the passer-by to wonder what was life really like living "down the lane", as ghosts of the past peer from guardian gates.'

The good people of Bridewell Lane can no longer invite us into their world, no longer warm our souls with laughter and song, but they are not forgotten.

Chapter 15
Up Cork!

Eddie Mullins

Eddie Mullins can thank the great Paddy Cotter for his introduction to the world of comedy theatre in Cork, at a time when every hall had a show and a packed audience to enjoy it. Theatre was the great escape for those who worried about the future: for an hour or two they could see the funny side of life up there on the stage.

When we met, Eddie spoke about that uncertainty and vulnerability of employment that existed in those days in the city and county.

> If you did not have a trade, it was hard. There were jobs for people with skills. The mainstays were Ford's and Dunlop's. If you were not with them, then you were scratching around. Across the river it was a job in Sunbeam Wolsey, little else.
>
> Moneywise, Dunlop's lost Ford's by a long way.

They paid twice the rate of what could be got anywhere else; they were the multi-national kingpins and had the tyre market to themselves in the Republic. They paid a levy of £1 to the Government for every tyre produced. They supplied all the Government bodies such as CIÉ and all the state agencies.

Ford's, in Eddie's view, was a precarious job. The problems were space and production. If the factory went full steam ahead there would be a stockpile, so production had to slow down. The first three months of the year were busy and then there was a slackening off. If there was a shortfall of Cortinas or Escorts in the UK, that was good for Cork as the plant could then assemble sixty cars a week, which in the UK context was not huge, but it was important for those employed in Cork. If there was over-supply, production would be shut down and the workers put on un-paid leave. Things were transformed eventually when a very imaginative director came in and changed things. 'I was in the production stores and fortunately we were the last to be hit, so we survived many a lay-off.'

Theatre got Eddie his job in Cork. Jim Stack had a next-door neighbour who worked in Ford's. At rehearsal one night Eddie told Jim that he was available for theatre roles, as he had no job. 'We'll have to do something about that,' he told me. He came back the next night and I had the job. I did the medical and I got into Ford's.

It was Paddy Cotter who recognised Eddie's passion for theatre and his advice was for the young man to go and see everything and to learn from those visits to theatre in all its forms. 'There was no TV then, but there were live stage shows all over the place. There were nine pantos in Cork and surrounding area. Money was tight, but the big leisure outlets were the dance halls, the cinema and theatre. I tried everything. With the amateur drama groups you'd spend six months rehearsing for one night's performance at a festival. I was in Stack's class in the School of Music. When I got my job in Ford's we were rehearsing a production of *Hamlet*.'

Stacky was afraid that it would not work commercially. All his plays were guaranteed full houses, but he was not so sure about the classic dark tale from the Bard. Needless to say it did work.

Off The Wall: A scene from Ali Baba *with (l to r) Eddie Mullins, Bob Carlile, Paddy Cotter and Carmel Summersgill*
(© Cork Examiner)

Eddie got his first break in comedy when he appeared in a minor role in a production directed by Tom Cuthbert at the

Palace. Then popular and successful writers Finbarr McCarthy and Michael O'Brien were looking for someone for *The MacBrien Revue* in May 1965 at the AOH.

It boasted a powerful cast: Billa O'Connell, Ann Brennan, Anna Grace, Charlie Kelleher, Paul O'Leary, Mary O'Donovan, Carmel Summersgill, Sean White, Con Murphy, The McTeggart School of Dancing, and violinist Michael Russell; with musical direction by Edna McBirney and stage management by Con Keating; scenery by Finbarr McCarthy and production by Michael O'Brien. Prices of admission were 3/-, 2/6, and 1/6 and the programme was 3d.

The *Up Cork!* revue was staged once every two years, at the AOH Hall with a panto version every year at Christmas. After his appearance in the revue, Eddie was cast in the panto, since Paddy Cotter was looking for a side-kick opposite Billa as the dame. It was made clear to Eddie that he was the straight man, he was the 'feed' for the brilliantly witty Paddy. Eddie recalls:

> He was a very clever comedian with an expressive, 'full-moon' face. He was in the mould of the English comic Bernie Winters. Paddy would take a line from the script and on paper it meant little, but he'd make it work. One scene had the two lads walking along a railway track and Paddy pointing to a spot: 'This is where my brother had the accident. When the train hit him, I found his hand on the right-hand side of the track and his leg on the other. His head was further down and his body was over there.' Eddie, the feed, asks: 'What did you do?' Paddy: 'I told him to pull himself together.' Audience collapses.

Eddie loved working with Paddy. 'Billa and himself had great timing. I became Paddy's partner on stage for the *Up Corks!* In those casts were Ann Brennan, Charlotte O'Byrne, Sean White and Mary O'Donovan as the country housekeeper who had an eye on the farm labourer, Charlie Kelleher. They were the ideal combination.

The *Up Cork!* and panto runs could be seven nights a week for seven or eight weeks. By the end, you'd hate it. Billa took an interest in each and every performance because any mishap reflected on the company. If you missed an entrance on Billa, you'd hear over the intercom, 'Well girls, did I ever tell you about the day I got married, walking down the aisle, with seven girls holding up my dress and there he was with seven nails holding up his pants.' That line of fill-in patter from Billa would mean that someone had missed their entrance. There'd be panic in the tiny dressing room. It happened me. When the stage-manager, Con Keating, dropped the back-cloth, the stage was so small in the AOH that you would get snarled up in the curtain and miss your cue – and that's what happened.

Up Cork! really worked in the intimate surround-ings of the AOH. The record-breaker of the series was simply about Ford's boxes. It was reckoned to be the best show of its kind ever seen in Cork. The storyline was that Maggie Murphy decided that she would like to have a holiday home as she lived down the lane all her life. She decided to buy two of the Ford boxes that brought in the assembly parts from Dagenham.

She was going to have a 'bundalow' in Crosser, by the sea. Paddy Conroy painted a backdrop of stacked Ford boxes. The set received a round of applause every night.

Paddy Cotter, Eddie Mullins and Sean White in Up Cork *1964*
(© Cork Examiner)

Up Cork! continued to pack them in until the new Opera House opened in 1965. First Billa, then Paddy, transferred to productions on the massive stage in the new theatre and *Up Cork!*, it was felt, had run its course.

But until that time we had winessed a truly a remarkable era for comedy theatre in Cork: *Up Cork!* at the AOH; *Swans* in the Father Mathew Hall; *Artful Dodgers* in the CCYMS; and pantos in every hall in Cork and county. The irony is that the burning of the old Opera House and the vacuum created over a ten-year period, from 1955 to 1965, had served to fire actor and audience enthusiasm for shows. It was an artistic ill-wind.

Eddie says that in the *Swans*, Paudie Harris played to the strength of a line-up that cast two hilarious couples opposite each other: Bill Mahony and Der Donovan as the husbands, matched by Billa O'Connell (for two shows) and Paddy Cotter as the dames.

The Swans of the Lee was staged at the Father Mathew Hall in May 1965 to help defray the £20,000 cost of repairs to the Trinity Church roof, damaged in a major storm. The cast was Billa, Bill Mahony, Bob Carlile, Paddy Cotter, Der Donovan, Ann O'Brien, Bobby Carlile, Donie Kenneally, with Charlie Kelleher and Eddie Mullins as the Corporation workers.

In a programme note to a *Swans Are Flyin'* production at the Opera House in November 1987, Paddy Cotter recalled the very first show in the Father O'Leary Hall:

> About eight people attended. One of Cork's foremost actors at the time, Rex Archer, visited the dressing room and told the dejected cast that he believed that they were on a winner. The ingredients, he said, were bang on – two families who were always at odds; two Corporation workers who always seemed in trouble; add a garda, plus a culchie or two; some good singing; and, as Rex said, 'We'd be home and dry.' . . . The scripts for the *Swans* always flowed from the gifted pen of Paudie Harris. The cast of any *Swans* would be in the region of ten people – all of them comedians – so at any time in the productions there were continuous laughter. It must also be said that the ad-libs from the cast were a vital part of any *Swans*,

always adding to the fun. Since Bill Mahony, RIP, has passed to his eternal reward, a new producer has to be found. This then is Noel Barrett's first production and it's being looked forward to eagerly.

In conclusion, a letter to 'De Paper' from a typical *Swans* fan says it all:

> Sir,
> Did somebody say that theatre in Cork is dead? The *Swans* opened at the Opera House last Tuesday night and I was one of hundreds who witnessed that this immortal species still flies high. In an age when an oul' laugh is a rare enough thing, this all-Cork troupe gives us our money's worth every time. Whether you're a plumber or professor, publican or priest, you'll see the Opera House theatre as it should be, alive and kicking. It deserves the support we show the boys in red on the hurling field – the folks on the boards train just as hard. Let's make them winners.'

The cast for that 1987 production had changed considerably from the original and it was: Noel Barrett and Pat Sullivan, Charlie McCarthy, Pakie O'Callaghan, Paul Dennehy, Ed Mullins, Mary Foley, Gus McLoughlin, Maurice O'Donovan and Christy Morris. Musical director was Maurice Healy and the choreographer was Carmel Sanquest, with set design by Patrick Murray and stage management by Dick Healy. Eddie Mullins loved his time on the stage and remembers with fondness that first encounter with the wonderful Paddy Cotter.

The panto Ali Baba And the Forty Thieves *broke box-office records during its seven week run at the AOH Hall in 1961. This group celebrated the achievement with a dinner at the Metropole Hotel. Included are the MacBrien writing partnership of Finbarr McCarthy and Michael O'Brien with Billa O'Connell in the middle of the front row.*

(© Cork Examiner)

Chapter 16
The Show Must Go On

Charlotte Byrne

They say Cork people can feel homesick when they reach the Lower Road. As Billa has said, every Corkonian, home or away, remembers where they were when the old Opera House was gutted by fire on the night of 12 December 1955. It was a horrible loss in the broad, artistic context, as it was a much-loved repository of dreams for the generations who had frequented its warm, inviting theatre.

It was particularly horrifying for those who had actually trodden its boards and now stood by helplessly, watching as it was reduced to a charred ruin. It was not, however, a disaster. Cork might be without its flagship theatre, but the miracle was that nobody had died.

Charlotte O'Byrne remembers it now as if it were yesterday

I was still one of Eileen Cavanagh's Tiny Tots. The main curtain was closed but we were rehearsing for the panto, *Sleeping Beauty*, on stage. I was in the middle of a little solo number. At the same time director Jim Stack was in a production meeting with some of the main players in the circle bar space.

A message came to Miss Cavanagh from Jim. Smoke had been discovered wafting around the upper bar area. Miss Cavanagh was told to get the children out of the theatre as quickly as possible. We ran up the stairs to the dressing rooms for our taps shoes, coats and other street clothes. As we did so, there was an iron door between the backstage and the auditorium and there was smoke swirling around it, into the wings.

I failed to find my taps and never did; they, too, were lost in the fire. We rushed down the stairs, out the stage door and into Half Moon Street. We lived in Mahony's Terrace, off Dominick Street. That night my father was wallpapering the front room. A neighbour told my father that there was a fire in the Opera House. He threw on his coat and ran along Camden Quay, still in his slippers. Remember there was no Christy Ring Bridge then. He saw me and gathered me up into his arms. I remember still that the sleeve of his short coat was inside out and hanging by his side.

Charlotte was only a toddler when she first took the floor.

I was just two and a half years of age when my grandmother, also Charlotte O'Byrne, from Turners Cross, brought me in the go-car to Eileen Cavanagh's dance classes in the old Gresham Rooms in Maylor Street. The lady on accounts for Eileen was Maureen Cotter, sister of Billa's wife, Nell. Accompanist was Edie Campbell, wife of Opera House manager, Bill Twomey. I was the youngest pupil and those around my age were all sitting in a circle as the others went through their paces. I was so young, I actually wet the floor and Edie, a friend of my mother, got a cloth and came to my rescue. For years after she'd say that she was the woman who had to clean up after me. That stays with me ever since. I became Eileen Cavanagh's prize pupil, getting all the little solo parts.

One of those was as a baby bear in *Goldilocks*, the 1949 panto at the Opera House. Charlotte had a contract and was paid, through her parents, five pounds a week. This covered the period of rehearsals and performance time. There was no extra money for the four matinees in the first week and the two matinees each week for the rest of the panto. The agreement was null and void for any days when someone such as the Pope, the President or the Taoiseach died (or during any other calamity: for instance an epidemic, war, lock-outs, and so on). Little Charlotte was in showbiz and loving it.

It would indeed take a disaster to stop this young girl taking to the stage. Charlotte was really a child star from the late 1940s, with appearances in *Red Riding Hood, Jack and the Beanstalk, Aladdin, The Three Bears, Ali Baba,* and *Cinderella*. She was certainly a child wonder – she even took part in a radio broadcast with the Cork Melody Makers in May 1947.

Once again we must refer to the incredible contribution made to the show scene in Cork by the writing duo of Michael

O'Brien and Finbarr McCarthy. They not only scripted some brilliant pantos, but were the creators of *Up Cork!*, which packed them in every time a new show was staged.

Big moment for little girl: Popular manager of the old Opera House, John Daly presents a prize to Charlotte O'Byrne with Nancy Wine on stage

The cast of *Up Cork!* demonstrates the strength and depth of this show that set so many records. Ignatius Comerford was Maggie Murphy with Donal Kenneally as Terence; Tadgh Foley was Lord Dripsey and his daughter, Deirdre, was Sally Kane; Norrie Long was Ellie Dan Tommie; Sean White was Hardnut; Tadgh Healy was Mangles; and Tom Cuthbert was Turnips. On stage, too, were Charlotte and Carmel Heaphy, Maureen and Betty McTeggart, the Shandon Belles, Carmel and Cecilia Manning, Mary McCarthy, Maeve O'Connor, and Georgina and Noreen Roche. Musical direction was by Edna McBirney; scenery by Patrick Conroy, with P. Morrissey as stage-manager; lighting was by C. Keating and J. O'Hea; and Ignatius directed the production himself.

MacBrien scripted many pantos and one in particular, *Babes in the Wood*, had an all-star line-up at the old Opera House. Ignatius Comerford was the main attraction, accompanied by Pat Egan, Hazel Yeomans, Charlotte O'Byrne, Carmel Heaphy, Chris Curran, Chris Sheehan, Cecil Sheehan, Paddy Blanc,

Gertie Wine, and Sean Healy with the Lehane Sisters, Maisie and Elsie. The Lehanes were decades before *Riverdance*, but their original costuming and general performance marked them as something special whenever they appeared. That show also boasted the Shandon Belles, the Cute Kiddies and the Tiny Tots, under the direction of Nancee and Eileen Cavanagh. Decor was by Frank Sanquest and direction by James Stack. All that and a speciality act too, with Terrax and Lady, a high-wire act from Switzerland. Those were the days.

In 1948 MacBrien presented *Aladdin* in the old Opera House. What an incredible line-up they brought together. Dame Twankee was played by Ignatius Comerford; Josephine O'Hagan was Aladdin; John Cahill was the Emperor of China; Gertie Wine played the Princess; and the Cotter Sisters were the Ladies in Waiting. Chris Curran was the Magician; Cecil Sheehan appeared as Yu Tu; Chris Sheehan was the Genie; and they were supported by James J. Nation, Peg O'Connell, Sean Healy, Rose Sheppard, Edna McBirney, Foster and Clarke. Music from the Cork Lyric Singers (J. Evans, T. Quinlan, W. Luttrell, D. Mullins and P. Mullins), the Shandon Belles, the Cute Kiddies, the Tiny Tots and speciality act, the Geddes Brothers, ensured it was a panto to remember for young and old.

It is interesting to note that the then manager of the Opera House, John Daly had asked Dickie Forbes to write a panto script with topical and local references in the 1930s and it was presented in 1936. MacBrien maintained that tradition in the 1940s.

Returning to Charlotte's own story, she says she recalls the arrival in town of Micheál MacLiammóir and Hilton Edwards with a production of *Liffey Lane*, which ran in May 1951 at the old Opera House. She remembers one amusing incident in particular. 'Stage-manager for *Liffey Lane* was a woman called Prepita and she picked me, with Kay Dowling, Pat Kidney and another girl, whose name I've forgotten, to perform as the children of *Liffey Lane*, with two lads chosen from the Echo boys. We were rowdy Dublin street urchins and we were paid a half crown a week.'

The youngsters made just two short appearances and had plenty of time in between, before their parents collected them early in the second act. The Echo boys left the theatre without permission, prior to their first stage call in the first act, to get a few bags of chips in the 'chipper' in Drawbridge Street. One of the lads brought a bag of chips down to the wings just before the 'urchins' went on stage. Prepita got a whiff of the chips and the young stars were fired. Miss Cavanagh was not too happy with her star pupils either.

When I was eleven I was attending the Fíor Gaelach Model School and I was in the famous Bean Uí Bhriain class, mother of Siobhán O'Brien, the wonderful cabaret and show performer married to Jack Riordan.

There were auditions for the Roy Croft touring show. Stars were Cecil Sheehan and Paddy Cassidy, whose stage name was Chuck Winters. I was chosen and we went on tour. I ended up going to school in Limerick, Lahinch and Waterford over the four months. I appeared in the shows at night. In the first half of the show I was Red Riding Hood with Cecil as my Granny. The second half was a variety show and a talent competition. When we were in the Savoy in Limerick, Patrick Begley, who had been let go by Radio Éireann because of his 'too' British accent, was on the bill. It was a big controversy at the time. Mr Begley was a lovely man.

Also in the show was an act called 'Silvio and His Harp'. It turned out that Silvio had hypnotic powers. When Charlotte developed a bad toothache, Silvio hypnotised her and the pain disappeared for a few days until she was able to get to a dentist.

After the show Charlotte went back to school at the Model, did her Primary Cert and got it, even though she had been away touring.

> Every Tuesday the famous Father O'Flynn would come in from Passage West. He introduced me to sean-nós singing. In the summer he brought me down to Ballingeary. He had the choir in Passage with Sr Teracita. One time the choir went to Dublin and they brought me along. We sang on Dún Laoghaire pier. [Charlotte was about twelve at the time.]
>
> I then went to St Vincent's Secondary and continued singing with Sr Mary Benedicta. I joined the School of Commerce Secretarial Class. A few months before my exams, I was diagnosed with tuberculosis and spent three months in Sarsfield's Court. After my recovery, my first job was with Harrington and Goodlass Wall. After five years I joined Sunbeam Woolsey.

Charlotte, a brilliant pupil, was now combining a successful career with a hectic on-stage life that had taken off in her teenage years. She was to become an integral part of some of the most successful stage shows ever produced in Cork. She performed in those brilliant MacBrien productions, including the 1960 show that broke all records. She recalls playing opposite tenor Donal Kenneally in 1962 and 1963 and she may have set a record by appearing in twenty-one *Swans* productions.

Swanning Around: Noel Barrett and Tony Hegarty vie for the attention of Charlotte O'Byrne in The Swans In Love

My first *Swans* was as the juvenile lead in the Opera House. I played several different parts, but I ended up as the 'country girl' in the role once taken by Peg O'Connell and I played opposite Christy Morris. The whole concept of the *Swans* was brilliant – it's no wonder they were so successful. The main characters we will never see on stage again. You could not really put on a *Swans* show now. The characters made the *Swans*.

Paudie Harris always knew who could make a particular line their own. He'd say: 'That's a Josie line; that's a Dolly line; and that is for Taigín.' He was always right, as he was very clever in his scripting. He left it then up to the actor to deliver and Bill Mahony was a smashing director. When an actor asked as to his or her exit movement, Bill would say: 'What way did you come in?' Given the answer, Bill would say: 'Then go off that way.' Oh! The fun we had in rehearsal.

I loved, too, my time with Collins Musical Society in the late '60s. My favourite role was as Wanda in *Rose Marie* . . . It ran from January 23 to February 7, in 1968. They told me that I stole the show. Collins was very professionally run with Commandant Bunny Kealy as the mainstay and Harry Bogan as director. Christy Whitnell was always brilliant in the comedy roles.

Charlotte O'Byrne

Charlotte also appeared in *Desert Song, Vagabond King* and *White Horse Inn*. That 1971 production swept the boards at the Association of Irish Musical Societies (AIMS) national finals, with Charlotte getting Best Supporting Actress and awards also going to: Chris Whitnell (Best Actor); Harry Bogan (Best Director); Pat Murray (Best Design); and Eileen Cavanagh (Best Choreographer). She adds, 'I directed Romberg's *Student Prince* for the Cork Operatic Society and we sold out at the Opera House. That show was very important to me.'

All this and three pantos for Fermoy in the Youth Theatre, plus cabaret nights with Tony Hegarty in Connolly's Hotel in Owenahincha; Charlotte has done it all. She has been associated with eight successful *Tops of the Town* productions: four of them with Sunbeam; two with Ford's; one each with Pfizer and Conna; and a spring show with Castlelyons Community Group.

Charlotte went to America in 1986 and stayed there until 1995, becoming involved with the American Corkmen's Association and other Irish groups. 'I missed Cork very much and when I came back I became PA to Clayton Love Jnr, one of the best jobs in Cork.' Shortly after her return Charlotte was back on stage in Michael McAuliffe's production of John Power's *As Some Tall Cliff.*

Charlotte is a co-producer, with Kevin Sanquest, of *Cork on Show*, and the five shows to date have been staged in support of Cork Cancer Research Centre. 'I'm singing with St Mary's Choir under the direction of Sean Lehane and I'm loving it. We've been invited to Knock for a big Dominican Order celebration.'

In her few quiet moments Charlotte O'Byrne looks back on her life so far and wonders: 'How did I do all that?'

A happy group in the old Opera House, probably the Circle Bar area perhaps some time in the late 1940s or early 1950s. Can you name all those in the picture? Identified here are: Nell and Phil Cotter, Gertie Wine, Eileen Donnelly, Carmel Hayes, Ronnie O'Shaughnessy, Charlotte O'Byrne, Pat O'Kane, Roberta Fitzgibbon, Maureen Cotter, Nancy and Eileen Cavanagh, Sarah Cotter, Eileen Heaphy, Dolores Kelly, Carol Levis and members of the Opera House staff.

Chapter 17
The 'Comerford' Zone

Paddy Comerford

As I was on my way to interview Paddy Comerford about his continuing impact on the Cork stage scene, I was thinking about his cousin, Ignatius Comerford, and his annual appearances on the Cork panto stage. It can be tricky these days to remember where I have left my car; so it is strange that, sixty-five years on, I can still recall in almost every detail my visits to the old Opera House on the St Stephen's Days of my childhood.

The whole house in Blackrock would be woken early in the morning by the Wren Boys knocking loudly at the door. There they would stand with blackened faces, furze branches in hands, gathered, no doubt, in Lakelands – once the disputed territory of our 'cowboys and Indians' days, now a shopping centre. At midday, a plate of cold turkey and stuffing, Hosford's buttered crusty bread, washed down by large glasses of creamy milk from Horgan's farm just across the road. Then off went myself and the younger brother, hand in gloved hand with Mam and Dad, to catch the double-decker bus at the top of Church Road.

A salute from the driver up in his lofty cab, free bus rolls from the singing conductor and, supported by puffing parents, we would scramble up the curved stairs to the shiny leather seats at the front, while hurtling past posh gardens. We would roller-coaster by Menloe Gardens, down to Ballintemple, up by Mary-ville, along Blackrock Road, swaying down Dead Woman's Hill, along Victoria Road and into the city.

We were going to the pantomime and we would have high tea later in the Cozy Café, with its linen tablecloths, on the Mall. Panto day was the best day of my childhood years.

Tickets bought, we would climb the steel steps clinging to the north wall. Out of breath with excitement, we would enter that wonderful old Opera House, a hall of mirrors and magic to lads from the 'country' in the big city. We were unaware then that Cork's favourite building would succumb to fire some ten years later; it seems our bright-eyed innocence would never be recovered from the ashes.

On one of those St Stephen's Day afternoons I first saw the man dressed as a woman. My parents would be talking about him for days and weeks before, and after, our Christmas outing to town.

The Comerford name is writ large across the billboard of Cork theatre. Ignatius Comerford, whose luminous stage career ended with a disabling stroke when he was just thirty-four, is remembered with deep fondness and warm respect. He was the truly great 'dame' for a generation of panto fans – the one whose illness robbed theatre of its Christmas star.

When Gay Byrne moved down to the audience in that memorable *Late Late Show* in 1982 to greet and pay homage to

Ignatius, I am sure that the memories of those heady panto times came flooding back, not only to the assembled stars in the studio in Montrose, but to thousands of old Opera House habitués watching that most popular of *Late Lates*.

Everyone, young and old, loved Ignatius. Young people find a lot to do when their attention wanders from the stage, so as children we spent whole scenes rummaging in sweet bags for the last Fort Brand caramels, or trying to prise the paper from the Cleeves toffee; but when Ignatius held the stage, we sat there hanging on his every word. It was his stillness, his quiet control of every situation, which I remember now. He was a consummate actor, as he demonstrated in other roles, light years from make-believe panto. He was the master of his craft whenever he played the 'mistress' of our pantomime world.

It must be in the genes. His cousin Paddy Comerford invites total attention from his audience by the merest self-deprecating shrug of a shoulder, the shy smile or a shuffle of the feet. And sometimes Paddy will just stand there, doing absolutely nothing, as an entire audience collapses with laughter. As with Ignatius, it is that same 'Comerford' zone.

Paddy thinks that his cousin's attractive power came from his ability to perform at the highest level in whatever role he took on. In fact many experts felt, such was his talent, that Ignatius would have made the big time if he had decided to leave Cork and follow theatre as a full-time career. Paddy's panto memory of his famous cousin defines the simple and effective artistry of the man, 'He'd move forward almost to the edge of the stage beneath the proscenium arch and play near the footlights. It was as if he was breaking through theatre's invisible fourth wall. It was his way of making a connection with his audience.'

The Dame (Ignatius Comerford) with the Babes In The Wood *(Hazel Yeomans and Olive Quinn) in the panto scripted by Dick Forbes*
(Cork Examiner)

Paddy remembers the night that Ignatius became ill after a panto performance in 1954, with just two more performances to go, matinee and night, before the end of the run. Ignatius wanted to go on and not let his audience down. His final performance was on the Saturday night and in the early hours of Sunday morning, he suffered a cerebral haemorrhage. It was as if a dagger had been thrust into the very heart of Cork comedy theatre.

Igantius battled through, but he would never again hold an audience in wonder and delight. His efforts to recover revealed a remarkable courage, and his presence in the studio audience that night in the *Late Late* was fitting for the man who defined the art of panto comedy.

Paddy recalls that awful time for the Comerford family and his legion of fans in Cork and surrounding counties.

> There were three years in the '50s that stand out in the memory for all Corkonians. In 1954, Ignatius became ill; in 1955, there was the 15-week drapers' strike in the city; and then, in '56, there was the outbreak of polio in the city. Early on in that strike there was an offer of a 15/- a week rise, but it was turned down. Some fifteen weeks later 15/3 was accepted.

> When Ignatius became ill, he was only thirty-four years of age. I remember my mother had given me two presents for his twin sons, Jack and Michael. I called to his dressing room in the Opera House. He had a desperate pain in his head. He told me that he had only two more performances to complete and he was determined to do so. In the early hours on the Sunday he was rushed to hospital.

His battle with his illness took him to Dublin and, eventually, home to his beloved Cork and the bosom of his adoring family. What might not be realised is that Ignatius never lost his love for theatre and Paddy recalls his always coming backstage after a panto or *Summer Revels*. When he did go to theatre, he would receive due mention from the stage. He was not averse to giving some gentle criticism of a particular script if he felt the need to offer it. In his time on stage, you had to invent your own brand of humour – there could be no references to TV, as it had not yet come on stream in Ireland.

Ignatius began his theatre days with the Red Abbey Players,

as did Peg O'Connell and Bill Mahony. 'Ignatius was a neat and tidy dame, thinner than Jimmy O'Dea. He was a lovely character actor away from panto. He was a very good mimic,' recalls Paddy. 'He appeared in the classic play, *The Hasty Heart*, and another about *Blessed Martin*, both directed by James Stack in the old Opera House.'

Paddy has a particular memory of seeing Ignatius and Chris Curran in an hilarious panto scene called 'Two to Tango'. 'Off stage he would mimic Auntie Madge and Auntie Molly. Ignatius as a dame had the style. At one stage the great J. F. McCormick was leaving the Abbey and Ignatius was auditioned to join the National Theatre. He was successful and the Abbey was his, but he decided to stay in Cork where he had a steady job and where he married Peggy Keating, rearing four sons, Paddy and Ignatius (both talented musicans), and the twins, Michael and Jack.' Illness brought heartbreak to Ignatius and his young family but he bore his suffering with tremendous dignity until his death.

Paddy Comerford, too, has known great sadness. In 1998 the death of his lovely wife Ann (née Madden) dealt him a heavy blow, which was to see his temporary disappearance from the stage much to the disappointment of his huge fan base. Paddy Comerford's name on a cast list is box-office security. When the Cork arts world paid tribute to my own work as Arts Editor of the *Irish Examiner* in 2004, Paddy made something of a comeback, though he was still feeling a deep sense of loss at Ann being taken from him. His performance almost brought the ornate Everyman Palace ceiling down on the packed house.

One storyline centred on the visit of Uncle Peter to a hospital accident and emergency unit. Peter told his audience that he felt that things were getting a little better for those unfortunate enough to have to use A and E facilities, though he did admit that not only were patients lying on trolleys – he could even see one inside a wheelie bin. It does nothing in the re-telling, but in the hands of Paddy it was a show-stopper, with audience and performers breaking up for several minutes. Another A and E story went like this: 'Is that you?' 'Tis' 'Sorry to hear you buried your brother.' And the caustic reply: 'I had to, he was dead.'

Paddy performed at the official opening of the Cork Arts Theatre and at the tribute evening at the Everyman Palace for the late Patrick Murray, scenic designer extraordinaire. Paddy simply sat on a stool, no dressing up, no props. He recalled his life and times, and the people with whom he had worked in theatre. It was mesmeric.

Paddy draws heavily on a wonderful childhood. When you meet and greet Paddy, it is as if you are entering his world, in which the most mundane and seemingly inconsequential happenings can be a source of great humour.

Take the story of King George, the much-loved and trusted donkey whose origins were in Bandon, but whose life was led in great comfort at the rear of Paddy's aunts' home in Ballymacthomas. Auntie Madge had a piggery – not unusual in those days. Twice each day King George, guided by one of a rota of drivers from the area, would pull a little cart down Nicholas Well Lane, on to Blarney Street, to the junction of Shandon Street (Gall na Spora) and down to North Gate Bridge, across the river, and up Bachelors Quay to the Mercy Hospital, where the kitchen waste would be collected as food for the piggery. Paddy's Auntie Molly incidentally was the first layperson to be employed by the Mercy Order. She was a secretary in the office.

Donkey King George would dutifully head back to Ballymacthomas and repeat the trip in the afternoon. Paddy had become part of the household since that day as a child when he had literally wandered up to the maiden aunts' house from his mum and dad's place. Paddy's staying at Ballymacthomas was undoubtedly a great comfort for his maiden aunties.

One day they decided that they would pay a visit to the family grave, at Curraghcippane near Clogheen, a few miles into the countryside. Uncle Stephen's splendid trap, complete with buttoned, red leather seating, was borrowed for the occasion. There was a royal problem. King George was a regular donkey and very set in his ways. His daily routine only ran to the twice-daily trips to the Mercy and back – and that was that. When he was pointed up Blarney Street to go west to the cemetery, he would not budge. It was decided to get him as far as the North Mall and, instead of crossing the bridge, guide him along the north bank of the river and up Sunday's Well. George said 'no', and stood his ground. A family outing to the country, and a chance for Paddy to display his pony and trap skills, had to be abandoned. As far as George was concerned, it was the Mercy mission only.

Paddy admits that he was once a 'one-hit' wonder starting out on the public performance circuit. Actually, it was a case of a one-vinyl record phenomenon – the record in question being a miming prop for gigs. On one side was Al Jolson's 'Sonny Boy' and on the other the Andrews Sisters' version of 'Sisters'. Billy Emery was in charge of the old 1978 record in its brown paper envelope. He was their 'roadie'. Paddy, Billy Kenneally and Jim Hastings were becoming a very popular mime act at the Sunday's Well Club on the Mardyke. 'Then stardom beckoned when we were invited to Muskerry Golf Club but there was an unforeseen problem – someone sat on the record on the way to the club.' Thus a major mime act had been shattered before it became really famous.

Paddy Comerford is best loved for his performances in panto and *Summer Revels*. He says:

> Panto is a very magical thing. The secret is sticking to the real storyline. There should be no gimmicks and no confusion for the four-year-olds in the audience. *Cinderella* should be every child's introduction to panto. In the best tradition of panto, all goodness should come from stage right [the Fairy Godmother or Fairy Queen] and all evil from the left [the Wicked Witch].
>
> My first experience was when Chris Sheehan asked me to play in *Julia's Magic Carpet* in the CCYMS Hall in Castle Street. Denis Harrington and himself used to call themselves the Artful Dodgers. Mary Cagney was the leading lady, with Edna McBirney as musical director. Joss Cahill was the dame, but because he was lecturing on the art of making stained glass windows in the School of Art, I was asked to step into his shoes. We did eight weeks. That was around 1960–61.
>
> I was then asked to play Buttons in the Father Mathew Hall with Siobhán O'Brien. Ann Brennan was Cinders. Comedy was supplied by the Hegarty Brothers, Neil and Tony, and Noel Barrett and Pat Sullivan were the Baddies. Direction was by Kevin Breen, with Bernard Geary as MD. It was *Cinderella*

again for my first panto at the new Opera House. I remember Mary Connolly, who had a beautiful voice, as Cinders, with James Stack directing.

Paddy was still in panto right up to the millennium year. He says, 'I did about thirty-six pantos in all. Funny, I never liked playing the dame in panto and did it just that once in CCYMS. Now playing the Ugly Sister was a different ball game for me.'

Devoted sisters Paddy Comerford and Billa O'Connell with baronial Da, Hardup, (Jim Queally) in Cinderella *at the Opera House, 1967*
(© private collection)

If you add in the fact that Paddy was an ever-present for twenty-two years of *Summer Revels*, you get some idea of his contribution to Cork comedy theatre. But there was even more to the man.

My first straight role in theatre was a walk-on part in John B. Keane's *Many Young Men of Twenty*. I was a character at the door waiting for the pub to open. I graduated to The Bird in Keane's *The Field*, with James N. as the Bull McCabe. I played in *Moll* with Mary O'Donovan as Moll. Flor Dullea and myself were the two curates and Chris Sheehan was the Parish Priest. Then there was another Keane, *The Crazy Wall*. I was the gadget player in Donal Giltenan's *Goldfish in the Sun*. I liked straight roles because sometimes there is need for discipline.

More recently Paddy returned to Keane again to play the county squire type in *Matchmake Me Do* for the Everyman Palace, directed by Michael Twomey. Paddy loved being Joxer in *Juno and the Paycock*, for which he got a Best Supporting Actor Award from the Cork drama critics.

Paddy has been compared to the great song and dance man Fred Astaire, so his involvement in some major musical productions should come as no surprise. 'Once James N. Healy summoned me to his hospital bed to ask me if I would take over the role of the Duke Of Plazatoro, which James was to play.'

Paddy did very well in the role at such short notice but he was surprised to find that the following night, James N. had made a remarkably rapid recovery and stepped back into the role. Paddy's fame in that show was short-lived.

'Another time I got a phone call from the Opera House at four in the afternoon, inquiring if I would be able to step into James N.'s shoes in his show *The Golden Years*. I was told to get my tea in the Oyster 'on the house', but I had little mind for tea as I was expected on stage in a few hours. I read the role from script sheets. I was on stage with a cast of Bill Golding, David McInerney, Ronnie O'Shaughnessy and all the stars of the Gilbert and Sullivan Group.

Again James N. recovered from his illness to take back his role the following night. Paddy maintains to this day that he was James N.'s best antibiotic.

Predictably, Paddy's favourite role in a musical was as the Strawman in *The Wizard Of Oz*. Dave McInerney was Tin Man and Dan Coughlan, The Lion. 'The first musical I was in was *The Belle of New York* for Cork Operatic Society. Then there was *Guys and Dolls*, in which I sang Nicely Nicely's 'Sit Down, You're Rockin' the Boat'. Now the company rule for that production directed by Jimmy Bellchamber, was that there were to be no encores. There were roars of 'more, more' from the audience and, rule or no rule, they had to get what they wanted.'

Crichton Healy wrote in his review of the performance that Paddy had brought down the house in his portrayal. The next night Paddy arrived at his dressing room to find his stage clothes outside the door. It was Dan Coughlan and Dave McInerney, his co-stars, jocosely saying, 'We've had enough of this star turn.'

There are fond memories, too, of Paddy's performance in the Father John Long directed *Hello Dolly*; and also the title role in *Fiddler on the Roof*, with James N. Healy, in which Paddy mimed playing the violin, with Frances Horgan doing the actual playing in the orchestra pit.

'Looking back now, I'm surprised at all the things I did do on stage. I was never trained. I never went to drama school. I loved movement. I loved Fred Astaire. I tried everything. I sang,

I danced, tried drama, panto, revue and tried to do all convincingly.'

His favourite directors include James Stack, Michael Twomey, Larry Oaks and Jimmy Bellchamber.

I've often thought that the fine art of being Paddy Comerford must have taken its toll in wear and tear on this most gentle of souls who has given so much happiness to so many in his myriad stage roles. Paddy does not admit to being very nervous prior to going on stage but says that he actually looks forward to it, especially when a show is into its run and going well.

> It never enters my mind that I would get a 'dry'. If I'm doing a solo performance, I'd have, say, five stories, but if a show is running for a while I'd change the running order, if only to entertain myself – but of course I'd always finish with the story that I had decided on with the stage-manager before going on stage.
>
> One of my favourite performances was in *Summer Revels*. It was the 'Continental', a big dance number with choreography by Larry Oaks. There was a darkened stage with spotlights on our feet only, and then the lights came up gradually on the whole stage.

Paddy, the great funny man, always loved Bob Hope. Other stars who lit Paddy's life were Marlon Brando, Marilyn Monroe and Simone Signoret.

In my continuing search for the secret ingredient in Cork humour, I asked Paddy if there were identifying characteristics.

> Take my Uncle Peter character. He is a cranky old

man, but he is also funny, because he thinks he knows it all, and because of this, he will often say the wrong thing.

Then there is the man who will short-cut everything. As MC at a singsong, he'll say: 'Noble call. Give us, Derisa. That could mean 'There Is a Flower that Bloometh', or, more likely, the Limerick rugby anthem, 'There Is an Isle'.

Then there is the disease that kills, and the know-all tells his buttie that it might be hereditary. When asked what does 'hereditary mean', comes the reply, 'It means this – if my mother and father couldn't have children, then I couldn't either.' When telling stories on stage, I'd build up the whole context to give greater impact to the tag line.

Paddy Comerford with his Cork Person of the Year award in 2004 (© Irish Examiner)

Paddy Comerford is certainly one of an élite group of performers who have no difficulty in moving from one stage discipline to another. He is most loved for his comic turns when Cork humour, for all its uniqueness, becomes the universal art of holding a mirror up to the human condition and being cheered and enriched by its reflection. A worthy entrant to Cork comedy's Hall of Fame.

Chapter 18
Man of Theatre

Charlie Ginnane

Charlie Ginnane never saw himself as a likely leading man. He has some very down-to-earth views about his own abilities as a stage performer, but in a long lifetime he has been a close, perceptive and engaged observer of theatrical history.

Educated first by the nuns in Passage West, he continued his primary and then secondary school education in the Christian Brothers College at Wellington Place. His earliest memory of theatre was the 1939 production of *Floradora* at the old Opera House, with Fan Cottrell in the leading role. There was, too, a production of *Rose Marie* in 1943 and a visit from the Carl Clopet Company. Even then Charlie was less interested in the actual performances, but more in learning about the technical and off-stage mechanics of theatre production.

The time, with its dulling awareness of war 'over there', and the rationing of basic goods, did not help a young man of seventeen looking for a job, but Charlie's tenacity was to pay off.

The imposing Munster and Leinster Bank premises at 66 South Mall was Charlie's first port of call one Saturday morning. He simply told the commissionaire, all imposing and posh in his green livery, that he wished to speak to the manager – a Mr Walsh. Charlie did get to meet the great man, who must have been impressed, since he arranged for Charlie to do the bank's entry examination the coming Christmas. Charlie did not become a banker, however, as he approached other companies, such as Cross and Co, Thompsons and eventually landed a job in Dunlop's. His dad worked next door in the millwrights department in Ford's. Charlie worked in Dunlop's for twenty-one years, until he joined Pfizer as a buyer and he would remain there for the rest of his working life.

Charlie never lost interest in the theatre world and recalls with fondness the Christians' Past Pupils Union drama and debating evenings. Lesley Horne and Don Bevan produced a version of John Bunyan's *Pilgrims Progress* with James N. Healy as Bunyan. In that cast were the brilliant Lorna Daly and a young actress, Maureen Fox, who would later become a journalist at the *Cork Examiner*, as well as appearing in some memorable plays. Also in the cast were Chris Curran, Dick Healy, Michael Beausang and Brendan McCarthy.

Joan Denise Moriarty was establishing her ballet school, which eventually became the Irish National Ballet Company. An annual problem was that she could never get enough male dancers for her productions. It should not be forgotten that Joan Denise composed her own ballets, based on such subjects as 1916 and Puck Fair.

Charlie had always wanted to play the role of Dr Copelius in *Coppélia*, but it did not work out. When Charlie was cast as the Burgomeister in the same ballet, the company's orchestral conductor, the legendary Aloys Fleischmann, suggested that Charlie might tap his staff on the stage floor in time with the music. 'Coordinating the movements with my baton, was how Professor Aloys put it,' according to Charlie. He did it, with difficulty.

Sartorial Elegance: (left) Charlie Ginnane in full costume for his role of Burgomeister in the ballet Coppélia; *and bewigged and quill at the ready in a scene from* Trial By Jury
(© (left) T. F. Sheppard)

Charlie recalls that in 1948 James N. Healy, who worked in the office at Ford's, was experimenting with wire recordings, combining dialogue with the Gilbert and Sullivan music on Decca recordings of classics such as *Patience*. Charlie is convinced that the James N. productions of *The Mikado* in 1951 and 1952 were some of the finest ever enjoyed on a Cork stage. Richard Mason had a rich booming voice as the Mikado and James N. was Koko, with Maurice McMahon as Poobah, Cyril Neville from Cobh as Nanki Poo, Mary Frost as Yum Yum, and Mary O'Meara as Katisha. Charlie says:

When the old Opera House was burned in 1955, it was like a death in the family but those first five years of the '50s had been wonderful in the context of Cork theatre. James N. lived Gilbert and Sullivan. He excelled as a performer in his own G and S productions, because he knew so much about the G and S tradition of production. He had studied in extreme detail the way in which the D'Oyly Carte Company, under the direction of Bridget D'Oyly Carte, daughter of Rupert, had modelled productions on the specification first laid down by Gilbert.

Ship ahoy! James N. Healy's artwork for the programme cover for a Nigel Hay production of HMS Pinafore.
(© James N. Healy)

After the fire at the Opera House all the companies were without their traditional base. The ballet company performed in the City Hall and the Gilbert and Sullivan Group appeared on the Palace stage.

Charlie had a long association with the John B. Keane plays, both as a stage-manager and an actor.

Sive was probably the most successful play in modern

Ireland. The number of groups who were staging it around the country was extraordinary. It was estimated that over 250 amateur companies either had it in rehearsal, on stage, or were about to tackle it.

In the first semi-professional run we did of *Sive* at the Father Mathew Hall, there were about one hundred performances. James N. claimed in later years that he had been in 500 performances of this John B. Keane classic about a young girl being married off to an old man.

Sive worked wonderfully, even though it was a fairly rough, rural melodrama. It seemed to catch the audiences and hold on to them. No other play did that to them in my experience. Nora Relihan and Margaret Dillon from the original Listowel Players production were Mena and Sive in our version. They had the true Kerry accents but the rest of us were at least fairly close to the county bounds. The older members of the audiences who came to see *Sive* in 1959 would have remembered Keane's depiction of rural ways and sayings. When Sive's grandmother, in one of her many clashes with Mena, says that she remembered when her people were 'drinking their tae out of jam pots', the audiences understood.

The Theatre of the South production did six weeks in Cork and then went to the Olympia in Dublin. *The Irish Times* critic of the time said that the production compared favourably with the plays presented in the early, golden days at the Abbey, which was praise indeed considering the Abbey had snubbed Keane.

The Listowel Players production did play the Abbey for a week after they had won the All-Ireland title in Athlone in that same year. It set the entire country talking about this upstart playwright from north Kerry.

On opening night in Cork, 29 June 1959, John B. said a simple 'thanks' to players and audience. Everyone present knew that something special had occurred and Irish theatre would not be the same after it. After the Olympia run, the company came back to Cork and it ran for another three weeks, then toured for that year all over Munster and returned to some venues.

The company members had their day jobs, so summer holidays were sacrificed for the trip to Dublin, with some members of the cast being unable to get time off. Charlie recalls being replaced by Frank Sanquest, the acclaimed Royal Hibernian Academy artist and brilliant theatre set designer, who sadly passed away at Christmas 2007.

Remarkably Charlie was just twenty-eight when he played the old man hoping to marry the young Sive.

> When I was leaving school I had this ambition to become involved in the stage, one way or the other. I thought I might progress from scene painting to design. Stage-managing did not appeal to me that much – it was more the artistic side of theatre production. If I could have secured parts in productions such as those being directed by James Stack, I'd have loved it. I was never the romantic lead type, in fact I did not fit easily into many roles, but if there was a Seán Dota type role – a crotchety type – then I was right for it.

With commendable good humour Charlie considers that his unfortunate car accident in the early 1970s fitted him ideally for certain parts. Charlie has ever since had to use a walking stick and he feels that he became perfect for any sort of 'one foot in the grave role'. In fact he played a character with two feet in the grave in *Our Town* in the old Cork Arts Theatre.

> I enjoyed appearing or working on the John B. plays because I liked them for what they were. I was both stage-manager and the old man dying in the bed in *Sharon's Grave*. I will never forget stage-managing *Many Young Men of Twenty*. In each performance forty drinks had to be served. The porter had to have a creamy head. That was great fun. The secret was burned sugar and water and I put a layer of cream on top. The chemists in Blair's and Lester's never asked what I wanted the burned sugar for. I also stage-managed *The Man from Clare*. When we got contracts it was even tougher, as I was not entitled to expect that anyone else would help with props or sounds off-stage. *The Man From Clare* was my favourite Keane.

I asked Charlie what he felt was the attraction and strength of Keane's work.

> In his early plays particularly John B. wrote about the things he knew about. He wrote about his Kerry. Remember, there is a place called Sharon's Grave. The thatcher in the play says he is going to check out if there is any work for him around Kerry Head.

Directly opposite in County Clare is Loophead, which is in fact Ceann Leime or Leap Head. In mythology Diarmuid abducts a willing Gráinne, their steed leaps across from that Ceann Leime to Kerry Head. In *Sharon's Grave* Neilus is obsessed with the whole legend of Sharon and her watery grave. It is a wonderful play, probably his best, better than *Sive*, and yet there are some wonderfully funny lines in it for all its darkness.

Charlie Ginnane may never have played the leading roles which he would have liked to have played as a young man, but his depth of knowledge and his assiduous attention to the detail of theatre ensured that he was vital to the overall success of so many memorable productions. He earned the reputation of being the most meticulous and dependable stage-manager in Cork theatre.

Chapter 19
Laughter and Song

Cork Musical Societies

Whenever comedy theatre in Cork is mentioned, it is understandable that shows such as the *Swans, Up Cork!, Artful Dodgers, Summer Revels* and the annual pantos are remembered with such ease.

However, it must not be forgotten that the many opera groups in the city ensured that it was not just serious classical music that filled theatres in Cork – there were also the comic operas and musical comedies which had audiences enthralled and theatre managers beaming from ear to ear, in spite of the fact that such productions have never been ready money-spinners.

One such group was the Cork Operatic Society. Founded in 1918, the COS presented a cascade of sparkling shows and celebrated sixty years on stage with a production of *The Student Prince* at the Opera House in 1978.

In an excellent programme note there was reference to the

changing face of the Ireland of that time. 'Natural gas is now piped from the ocean to Cork homes; Cork hurlers are in the process of winning three All-Irelands in a row; nuclear power is being mooted but resisted for the Carnsore site in Wexford; and Munster has beaten the mighty All Blacks in Thomond Park.'

The writer contrasts all that with those first tentative steps of the Operatic Society in Cork at a time when war clouds were slowly evaporating over continental Europe. In those dark times the Warblers singing group, with Danny Hobbs in their midst, kept spirits high in a city which had always welcomed the great opera companies to the old Opera House stage.

The Warblers Musical Group with the great Danny Hobbs front row, extreme left.

The very first COS show, *La Mascotte*, did not do well and the society's share of the box office amounted to just £166 7s 5d. It is interesting that the writer of the programme notes put down the small attendances to the fear of conscription in this British-ruled city that would become the second city of the Republic. *La Mascotte* was reprised as *The Luck Bringer*, but this time the dreaded 'Black' 'flu damaged the box office and the 'take' was even less.

The Gilbert and Sullivan favourite *The Gondoliers* did well and then it was the turn of *The Mikado* in 1920 – but on the Saturday night of its run the city was in flames, torched by the Black and Tans.

The COS had another date with destiny in December 1955, when they presented *The Belle of New York* – it was to be the final show presented on the old Opera House stage before that disastrous fire. Undismayed and determined to stay afloat, they headed for the Father Mathew Hall and productions of *The Quaker Girl* and *A Country Girl* in 1956 to mark the refurbishment of that theatre, which was to prove so vital to Cork theatre groups, the visiting Carl Clopet Company and, later again, the home of the Everyman Theatre Company. In *A Country Girl*, Michael Twomey was taking his first musical role as the leading baritone role opposite Noelle Callanan. It was a comedic triumph for Chris Whitnell.

COS headed for the Palace in 1958 to present a string of great musicals including: *Oklahoma*, which a critic described as 'hitting a new level of amateur musical performance'; *Finian's Rainbow*, with guest star Milo O'Shea; and a particularly memorable *Annie Get Your Gun*, with Mary O'Donovan playing a scintillating Annie Oakley.

It was entirely appropriate that the COS would be represented in the star-studded cast of that night in November 1965 when the new Opera House opened its doors in the presence of the President of Ireland, Éamon de Valera. Mary

Cagney and Chris Sheehan sang songs from the light opera and musical comedy repertoire.

The things theatre companies have to do to keep the show on the road or at least on the local stage! In 1973 an excellent *Paint Your Wagon* did not set the box office alight and it took almost three years for the Society to get back on the boards. Fund-raising included carol singing, revues, concerts, raffles, and support from benefactors and 'an understanding bank manager'.

Aideen Crowley Dynan is another fine example of the multi-skilled practitioner on the Cork theatre scene. A talented musician, teacher and director, Aideen not only produced the COS's Diamond Jubilee shows, *Merry Widow* and *Student Prince*, but choreographed as well.

These are just a few of the highlights in the life and times of an amateur group that refused to get off the stage when the odds and the doomsters suggested that they should. The COS survived the aftermath and fall-out of a world war, the turmoil of a civil war, uncertain times as the country struggled and found its feet – and then, when freedom and independence eventually came, there followed another world war and the economic upheaval wrought by a ravaged Europe.

Only the vision and spirited resilience of true theatre people could have kept the company going through such trials – and this is without the sheer uphill battle, at the best of times, involved in putting on a major production. The city is forever indebted to all amateur groups who dare to get on stage, put a song in our hearts and a smile on our faces by their efforts.

*

The Gilbert and Sullivan Group entertained Cork audiences from 1951 until 1980, driven with creative zeal by James N.

Healy. The final years' productions were *Cascade of Memories* and a full production of *HMS Pinafore*

In the opening year *The Mikado* and *The Yeomen of the Guard* were presented, followed by *Mikado* and *Iolanthe* in the second year. The group built up a large and loyal following through their dedication and consistently strong performance of all the G and S favourites, including: *The Pirates of Penzance, The Gondoliers, Trial by Jury, HMS Pinafore, Patience, Utopia Limited, The Sorcerer, The Merry Widow, The Student Prince, Lilac Time, Die Fledermaus,* and *La Belle Hélène.* There was also a pearl necklace of musical hits including, *Fiddler on the Roof, Oliver!* and *The King* and I.

An interesting familial link with the Gilbert and Sullivan Group is Declan Townsend, retired lecturer at the String Department in the Cork School of Music. Hs son, Brendan, who studied in Maastricht, Holland, is conductor of the Laredo Philharmonic in the US, and the fourth generation of conductors in the family. His great grandfather was Yorkshire man Arthur Townsend and his son was Luke Clifford Townsend who came to Cork as a British civil servant at the Income Tax Office. In what could be described now as a remarkable act of ecumenism, Luke, a Protestant, was heavily involved with the musical society at Father Mathew Hall, run by Capuchins, An tAthair Micheál and Father Columbanus. He later transferred to Tralee from 1927 to 1950, where he was deeply involved with the Tralee Musical Society. On his return to Cork, Luke was Choir Master at both the Methodist Chapel and the Holy Hour Choir at the Reparation Convent. In 1960 he conducted the Nigel Hay production of *The Merry Widow* at the Palace Theatre in Cork and his son Declan was Chorus Master.

When Luke became ill that year, Declan was musical director

for a production of *The Student Prince*. Declan conducted *The Mikado* which was the first musical to be staged in the new Opera House. His work with G and S included *Lilac Time, Iolanthe, Die Fledermaus, La Belle Helene, The Mikado* and *Gondoliers*. Declan also worked with James N. Healy on Christian College productions of *The Mikado, Pirates of Penzance, HMS Pinafore, Yeomen of The Guard* and *Patience*. and also found the time to conduct choirs from the Cork School Of Music, Irish Steel, The Hardebec Singers and in Macroom. Declan reckons that he has conducted over forty-seven performances of *The Mikado* in his career. He celebrated his seventieth birthday in 2008 when a special performance of his magnificent work *Aisling* was performed by an orchestra which included sons Peadar and Finbar, conducted by Brendan. It marked the incredible music legacy of the Townsend family.

A sumptuous scene from Die Fledermaus. *Note the ornate ceiling from which hang chandeliers, a feature of Patrick Murray's design*

*

Collins Musical Society made a remarkable contribution to the cultural life of the city from 1964 to 1975. In 1995 Captain Paddy Kelly, assisted by Chris Whitnell, researched the history of the Society. They re-recorded material on old spool tapes and presented their work to the Collins Military Barracks Museum in June 1996.

Army man Paddy Kelly has always been associated with the Society and is blessed with a wonderful voice, which he put to magnificent use during his musical stage days. Myself, RTÉ's Maire Ní Mhurchú and Captain Paddy were privileged to adjudicate the hugely popular over-60s competition finals, organised by Paddy O'Brien. Captain Paddy was the informed and calming presence when decisions had to be taken after nights of great entertainment in the Savoy, the Opera House, and then the City Hall.

Mary Sheridan and Charlotte O'Byrne in costume for Collins Musical Society's Rose Marie

At a meeting in Collins Barracks in 1963 it was decided to form a musical society. The commanding officer at the time was Colonel W. Donagh who had been associated with the Curragh Musical Society. Col Donagh became the first president of the Collins Musical Society, with Lt Col T. McDonald acting as chairman and Captain R. B. Kealy as musical director. *New Moon* was the Society's first production at the Father Mathew Hall in 1964, followed by *The Desert Song* at the same venue in 1965.

The Society's first production in the new Opera House was *Show Boat* in 1966. That venue was Collins Society's home for the next nine years, with productions including *Naughty Marietta*, *Rose Marie*, *The Vagabond King*, *The Desert Song*, *White Horse Inn*, *Bless the Bride*, *Land of Smiles* and finally, in 1975, a reprise of *Show Boat*.

*

Cork Operatic Society, the Collins Society and Nigel Hay Productions – as well as many more semi-amateur or professional groups – showcased many talented people. We must not forget, too, the incredible efforts of John O'Flynn and Donal O'Callaghan in their founding of the Irish Operatic Repertory Company, and particularly its associated Academy for young performers and although, while outside the scope of this book, the achievement of companies such as Cork Grand Opera and Cork City Opera are worthy of note, the latter led energetically and bravely by Pat Dawson.

The massive contribution made by the Montforts under the direction of their founder, Eileen Nolan, should also be remembered. Father John Long, a native of Cork, returned from the US each year from 1978 to 1992, from 2000 to 2005, and again in 2007, to direct a string of great shows for the Montforts. He directed: *Pippin*; *West Side Story*; *Hello, Dolly!*; *Oklahoma!*; *No, No, Nanette*; *Camelot*; *The Music Man*; *An Evening of Noel Coward*; a Gershwin–Lloyd Webber show; An Evening Of Rodgers and Hammerstein; *I Can Do That*; *The*

Best Little Whorehouse in Texas; Anything Goes; Oliver!; The Wizard of Oz; Proof; Magic of the Musicals; and *High School Musical.* For some years now Father Long has made Cork his home again, and he can point to his terrific record as the driving force of the Montforts for so many years, ably supported by their Musical Director, Ronnie O'Shaughnessy, Valery O'Leary, who directed *Steel Magnolias* in 1992; Marion Wyatt (*Gingerbread Lady,* '95); Trevor Ryan (*Our Day Out,* '96); David Gordon, (*Jerry's Girls,* '95) and Karen Hackett, (*Seussical,* 2008)

Paint your wagon with Dave McInerney, Finn Scannell and cast.

Dramatic theatre found expression, too, when members of the St Vincent's Church Choir helped form the Well Players.

The Players included Bill Mahony, *Swans* director Michael McAuliffe and Tommy Dynes. Michael was mesmeric as Michael Collins in G. P. Gallivan's *The Stepping Stone* and played Collins again for RTÉ's 1916 Commemoration series. Tommy was, of course, an ever-present in the *Swans* series, as well as a panto favourite. Also at the Well were Lorraine Jones, Mary Kerrigan, Bill Hammond, Der O'Donovan, Henry O'Mahony, Sean Riordan, John Cambridge, Kay Collins and Jim Bevan.

I cannot imagine how grey our lives would have been without the efforts of these people bringing the best to local stages – the temptation at times must have been to fold tent, strike the set and close the stage door for good. They lit up our lives with their brilliance and we must never forget them.

Chapter 20
The Fascination of Chaplin

Chris Whitnell

Charlie Chaplin fascinated Chris Whitnell. Son of a cinema-projectionist father, it was little wonder that the boy who had a free pass for the Pavilion and Lee Cinemas in Cork would want to emulate his screen idol and make people laugh. He achieved his ambition – and his golden moments certainly came 'centre stage'.

Chris loved Chaplin's sense of mimicry and the way that he created original characters without resort to words. Chris is best remembered now for his own interpretation of the comic roles in the musical genre. If there was laughter to be mined from the lines, then Chris was the one to make the most of them.

A Sullivan's Quay boy, he remembers a production of *Ali Baba* and some of the school friends who appeared in that production, including Daithi Ó Sé, Paul Rispin and Brendan Buckley. Chris was Captain of the Thieves. Accompanist was Miss M. Power, with costumes for the Ladies' Chorus designed by Violet Cummins and executed by Gings of Dame Street, Dublin.

Billy and Julia Whitnell always encouraged their son's interest in the stage, though his father might have wished that Chris showed more interest in sport. Tower Rovers, one of the more famous youth soccer clubs in the country, came into being when Chris' dad saw the children of their area making do with a rough patch of ground at the back of Mercier Park in Turners Cross, near the old railway line.

Chris remembers that after the 'match' they'd cool down in a stream known as 'back of the Bandon', a reference to the old Bandon Railway. Billy Whitnell convinced AOH to support a youth club for the lads and Tower Rovers was born.

Although cinema was special to Chris – his father was projectionist at the Pav for forty-nine years and his uncle, Timmy Murphy, was projectionist at the Lee Cinema in Winthrop Street – very soon he was attending drama classes conducted by Lorna Daly. In fact theatre was in the family too, as his uncle, Paddy Murphy, had a fine baritone voice and sang in Father O'Leary Hall. Paddy's brother-in-law was the fine tenor Donal Kenneally.

> I fell in love with my teacher Lorna, and attended her classes for years. When I directed *Tons of Money* at the Father Mathew Hall in 1956, Lorna played my wife. Lorna directed a version of *The Playboy of the Western World* and we were rehearsing in the CCYMS when the old Opera House went on fire.
>
> We were all crying down by the Dominican Church as we saw all our theatrical futures going down the Lee. Lorna was a great teacher because she

got the best out of you by giving you encouragement.

Down the years I was very lucky with directors, including Gertie Counihan, Mavis Shrubb and Nancee Cavanagh, who directed me in *Belle of New York*.

Chris toured his own production of *Tons of Money* when he was just twenty. Father Buckley, of Coachford panto fame, invited the company to play in the local hall. Chris remembers that there was a big Munster hurling match that day, so they were not expecting a big house. He thinks Father Buckley anticipated this and invited families of the travelling community to join the audience and the show was a box office success.

There was a real sense of ecumenism in the Cork theatre community of the time. The National School is now gone, but at that time was attached to Christ Church, where Bishop Lucey Park is now. Chris and others often rehearsed plays in its white stone building and, in recognition of the courtesy afforded to them by the Protestant Church, Bishop Simms was invited to a performance of *Tons of Money* in the Cork Catholic Young Men's Society Hall in Castle Street. In the play there is a scene where an explosion occurs through the detonation of maroons. This time the blast blew out the windows in the CCYMS. Fortunately, His Lordship and those in the audience were unharmed. Good relations were maintained.

A fire in a building which stored sets and props in Carey's Lane meant that a charity tour to Sarsfield's Court, then a TB unit, looked like being cancelled. Not a bit of it – Chris and the group made do with a setting of screens and hospital beds and the stage was a set of tables. The show went on!

Christmas Days were spent putting on shows in what was then known as the Blind Asylum; afterwards the troupe would move on to the South Infirmary, Victoria and St Finbarr's Hospitals. On the hospital tours, Chris and Seanie Carroll would do a cross-talk routine, giving old, dated scripts a new lease of life.

Troubadors: Chris Whitnell, Charlotte O'Byrne and Noel Murphy in a scene from the Collins Musical Society's The Vagabond King
(© John O'Reilly)

Chris, whose day job was in Dunlop's, has the distinction of performing with all the main musical groups, including Collins, Cork Operatic and Nigel Hay Productions. He always had a 'thing' for comedy. He loved appearing in all the great shows such as *Oklahoma!, Show Boat, Naughty Marietta, Rose Marie,*

The Vagabond King, *White Horse Inn*, and so on. He was almost an ever-present with Collins Musical Society. They described him as 'one of their own', so popular was the young man whose comedic timing, sense of energy, and fun made him an explosive presence on stage and a huge favourite with audiences.

Chris was not above making changes to a script when he thought it was needed, having first checked with the director of the show. 'In *Show Boat*, as Cap'n Andy, I had to slag off the Irish Navy. That day, on a conducted tour of the harbour, a depth-charge blew up too close to the boat. There was a valve rupture and a fire broke out.' There was a change to the script in that night's performance and the incident got a mention. In character, Chris was asked, 'What's coming up the river?' and the new response was, 'As long as it is not the Irish Navy.' The audience loved it.

Members of the cast of Show Boat *with Chris Whitnell (front extreme right)*

Chris was in constant demand and he appeared in a James Stack-directed production of B. G. McCarthy's *The Whip*

Hand, with Kevin Sheehan, Lorraine Jones, Bill Mahony, Der Donovan, Heather Underwood, Pat Horgan, Pat Fenton, Assumpta Wallace and Evelyn O' Hanlon. Another James Stack production was *Not in the Book* in which he played the son, Michael; then there was Rex Archer's production of *Shinny's Men*, with Brendan Fehily, Ann Neeson, Lorna Daly, Mon Murphy, Dan Coughlan, Donal Donovan, Tadgh O'Sullivan, John O'Shea and Vincent Twomey. That was followed by *All the King's Horses*, directed by James N. Healy, with Kay Healy, Mary O'Donovan, Michael Twomey, Donal O'Donovan, Charlie Ginnane, Irene Comerford, Bernard Power, Michael McAuliffe and Flor Dullea.

Chris was visiting lovely Ardmore village in County Waterford when he first heard the Hennessy ballad group from Wales – he was to become their manager here. 'By the time they finished in Ireland, I had got my brother-in-law, Sean O'Hanlon, to teach them Irish. So now they were singing not only in Welsh, but also in French, English and now Irish.' At the opening of the Sunset Ridge Hotel in Killeens they appeared on the bill with Patricia Cahill.

Chris loved comedy but did not like pantos. 'I liked character comedy. I did just three pantos – two were in the Father Mathew Hall and one in the Opera House. I found, as a married man with a young family, that pantos made such demands on your time at Christmas. You'd be rehearsing on Christmas Eve. If things were not working out, you'd have to go back into the theatre on Christmas Day for more rehearsal. Rehearsals started too late in December. No, panto was not for me.'

In 1969 Chris agreed to direct a play, *Children in Uniform*, for the Sacred Heart Convent in South Douglas Road. Eileen Nolan of Montfort fame was involved. Chris' sister-in-law,

Evelyn O'Hanlon, led the cast and they went on the drama festival circuit. They had great success, winning a Best Play award, a Best Actress award for Evelyn, and a Best Producer award for Chris.

Looking back, Chris considers his happiest and most fulfilling time was on the musical comedy stage. 'I loved musicals, as you always had a good chorus and fine individual performers. I was fortunate to be directed by Lt Commander Liam Smith from Haulbowline, and by Harry Bogan, too, a good and gentle man. Performing with Collins was a real social event. I did *The Belle of New York* with Cork Operatic Society in '55 – the last show in the old Opera House. I worked a lot with COS, including *Oklahoma!* at the Palace in '57.'

Then there was a succession of appearances with Collins until the 1972 rehearsals in the CCYMS for *Land of Smiles*, when Chris suffered a major heart attack and was rushed to the Mercy Hospital. It was three days before Christmas. After recovery, medical advice recommended no more stage work. Chris put so much into his performance on stage that there was no way he could ignore the advice.

An example of the wear and tear on such an energetic and spontaneous performer was the 1969 production of *The Vagabond King* in the Opera House. Each night he had to dive into a barrel specially made by a cooper in the Beamish and Crawford brewery. The barrel was padded, but Chris was black and blue after each show. The whole thing was a love affair between Chris and the stage and now it was over. Well, not quite.

'In '75 I produced the *Tops of the Town* show for Carrigaline. I did it again in '77 and at the outset I knew that we had the makings of a national title winner, and in fact we had. The winning team included Jack Brierly as musical director and Noel McCarthy as choreographer. Mai Murphy, a first cousin, was the soprano. We beat Aer Lingus in the final in the Gaiety.'

Chris seldom goes to theatre now as he feels that if he identified with a particular role, it would all be too intense and emotional for him. However, he can say that he gave every part his best shot and entertained us all in the process.

Chapter 21
Heaps Of Slag

The Slag Revue

Cork County Council now has a very progressive and active Arts Office, but in the 1950s and 1960s it did not exist. However, there were two creative forces within the Council staff.

The late Colum Fehily, writer, and Donal O'Donovan, producer, were the bright sparks behind one of the most popular satirical shows ever to take the stage in Ireland. The *Slag* shows are still remembered by those who were lucky enough to crowd into the little Group Theatre in South Main Street.

My inside track on the 'Slaggers' came from Donal. It was clear that any book about comedy theatre in Cork had to include this all-important series that skittled all of Cork's most sacred cows, from the business suits on the Mall and the sailing class in Crosser, to the 'impecunious' farmers – not forgetting the forces for law and order. Nobody was safe and that 'nobody' was probably in the audience anyway, if he or she could get a ticket.

Former Council colleagues knew about the talented Mr Colum and Mr Donal, since their impromptu sketches would be tested in the office (outside office hours, of course) before the lads went public in the Group.

Donal remembers his time in the Council well and he admits that he had a talent for mimicking some of the characters working around him. There was always the hooley at staff parties to mark a marriage or a retirement and Donal would do his party piece 'just for the laugh, nothing serious'.

Slaggers All – Donal O'Donovan, Charlie Hennessy and Michael Twomey at the Gala Anniversary Concert in the Opera House in 1995

> I wasn't interested in authority work at all, it was just a job. It was the mid-1950s and around that time, while I had no formal training, I was always tinkling

around with a piano at home. I eventually got a job with the Johnny Byrne Showband. We wore red blazers, white pants, Rubber Dollies (leisure shoes) and club ties. We stood on stage and I had to stand sometimes too, although I was playing the piano. One night we were the relief band for Victor Sylvester Jnr and his orchestra at the Arcadia. Victor was on the main stand, which was at a lower level than the relief stage at the other side of the hall. It was a strict tempo, with Victor waving his baton and beaming to the assembled dancers.

Victor then handed over to us and Johnny dispatched me to the drums and he proceeded to 'conduct' the band in our opening rock 'n' roll number. Strange as it may seem, the punters much preferred the stuff we were playing.

Apparently Victor was not impressed and said as much to the proprietor, Peter Prendergast.

One evening in the Star Ballroom in Millstreet Donal decided he had enough of the showband scene, triggered, it seems, by a request for the Cliff Richard hit of the time, 'Please Don't Tease'. It was not just the song but the whole dance scene that was getting to Donal. The late nights, shifting the gear, and then getting up the next day for the day job all got too much and, as it happens, Donal was taking a step in the right direction.

Now in our late twenties, colleague Colum Fehily suggested that we should go to the drama class in the School of Music. I loved the drama and Colum was a great man with words. Because we were mature students, we'd have a drink afterwards with the maestro himself, James Stack, in Heaphy's pub. Colum loved the flow of the conversation. Michael McAuliffe would drop in and I remember Chris Collins and Mairín Murphy.

My first role was a compère for James Stack's *Holiday Revels*, which Stacky had been doing for years at the Father Mathew Hall. It starred Billa O'Connell, Ann Brennan, Bill Mahony, Peg O'Connell and many others.

My first real part was in a play called *Not in the Book*, a comedy thriller. I was a South American blackmailer, Pedro Juarez, and Lorna Daly played the wife and I think Michael McAuliffe played the lead.

Donal actually 'died' on stage every night. Linguist John Foley taught Donal some vituperative Spanish that loosely translated into: 'The desire to live is strong but you [the heart] are weak. I say this to you: f**k you for a heart.'

I asked Donal what he felt was James Stack's gift. 'He gave us absolute confidence. He told you what to do and how to do it and you went on with complete confidence in yourself. He was absolutely sure of what he was doing. When he arrived at rehearsals, everything was plotted in advance to the millimetre. Where you stood, each move, everything was accurate. He was part of the Father O'Flynn legacy at the Loft.' Donal was earning his crust by day, but was now waiting for the night when theatre became a way of life.

The Southern Theatre Group (Dan Donovan, Frank Sanquest and James N. Healy) presented John B. Keane's *The*

Highest House on the Mountain; it was the first time that Donal had worked with Michael Twomey. The John B. Keane classic plays had already been done first time around, but Donal did appear in some of the revivals. Of the origins of *The Slag Revue*, Donal has this to say:

> Colum was very aware of my penchant for mimicry and he felt we should get together and do something. Colum was a native of west Cork, attending Castletownkinneigh National School. He was young when his family moved to Cork. He went to the North Monastery. I went there after I had finished in Sullivan's Quay. He got his literary flair from his parents. He was very fussy about his Christian name, Colum, and his birth cert said 'Patrick Colum Fehily', after the poet Padraig Colum.
>
> With regard to the scripts, I'd leave Colum off and he later showed them to me, and invariably I liked them. I'd make suggestions but they were all his work.
>
> We wondered where we would put on a show like the *Slag* and we headed for the smallest theatre in town, the Group Theatre or, as it was known, Healy's Hall after James N. Healy. I was friendly with Michael Twomey and he suggested Charlie Hennessy. They were former Pres boys and the North Mon man Colum was hoping that they would do justice to the scripts – and they did. Charlie used his mother's maiden name 'Stenson', so he was cast-listed as Cathal Stenson, as the Law Society would not be crazy about one of their own taking part in a *Slag* show. I felt also we would need a musical interlude

so we were joined by Siobhán O'Brien. She had a fine singing voice and sang in the cabaret style for the shows.

We had only one wing space to change between sketches. We prepared, adopting a theatre workshop approach, with Colum always present with the cast and with me as director.

Donal believes that the *Slag* shows were a first by a local company.

I was influenced by shows I had seen in the Pike Theatre with Milo O'Shea and Des Keogh. I was very aware of the intimate review genre. I had seen Edith Piaf in the Olympia in Paris in 1956 and I asked Siobhán to do a set of her numbers, which she did beautifully.

We weren't sure how Establishment Cork would take to the shows. It was really trial and error. Some stuff we knew would go down well, but we also tried items that were open to question as to their reception. They were not for general audiences and so we might lose them, but we took the risk. We satirised the new wave, the whole cult of Shakespeare and contrasted attitudes in revolutionary Ireland with our time.

Our audience were in the main the very people we were satirising. We were the first to articulate what we would call the Cork 'fruity' voice with a character named George. There were a lot of 'Georges' wondering was it someone else or was it them? Every 'George' in town came to see the show.

All the sketches were different. We did one show a year and they continued for just about three or four years. I think the first was near the end of '61 and the last some time in 1965. Casts included: Charlie Hennessy, Michael Twomey, Donal O'Donovan, Mary O'Donovan, Denis O'Donovan, Siobhán O'Brien, Joss Cahill and Charlie Ginnane who also stage-managed. Piano accompanist was Clare Egar and sound effects were by Denis O'Donovan, with some original sets by Harry Wallace.

Colum's strength was his ability to zero in on a subject and get to its core and then saying it as it was. His writings told you everything about what the man was about.

Donal feels that the reason the *Slag* shows came to an end was that they felt there were no more sacred cows to knock over. Like *Fawlty Towers* they seemed to have been there forever, so great was their impact, but in effect there were just three or four 'Slags', with a special benefit show in the 1970s in aid of the Everyman.

In 1972 Donal was in the cast of actors who headed off to San Francisco, invited by the United Irish Societies of San Francisco. An Irish American woman, Mrs Quilter, played host to the Theatre of the South Company. 'We stayed on the Lone Mountain College Campus. We did *Sive*, which I was in, and there were also performances of *The Year of the Hiker* and John Murphy's *The Country Boy*, and James N. Healy presented his one-man show.'

Into the dressing room after the first night of *Sive* in the Bishop Kearney Theatre, came a childhood pal of Donal's, Jack

Falvey from Boreenmanna Road. He had not seen Jack since he had emigrated to the US. They celebrated well at Jack's house before the night ended and Jack's son drove back to the college with Jack and Donal very happy about an unexpected reunion.

Illness in the 1990s ended Donal's connection with theatre, but his trips down the Marina and out by Blackrock Castle on his motor bike help to fill his day and evenings are happily spent listening to radio and his music collection. The *Slag* shows and his memories of working with the genius that was Colum Fehily still warm his thoughts.

Chapter 22
Renaissance Man

Charlie Hennessy

Renaissance man Charlie Hennessy was a 'Slagger'. He believed he was, in effect, the first Cha to Michael Twomey's Miah. A senior partner in a reputable Cork legal firm, Charlie Hennessy did a name change all those years ago in the 1960s and became Cathal Stenson in order not to attract the attention of clients to his nightly efforts on the little Group Theatre stage. The 'Stenson' came from his mother's side and Cathal, if you like, reflected his love of the language.

The *Slag* shows were his theatrical swansong, at least from a performance point of view, though his love of the art continued to find fruitful association, as he has been the inspirational Chairman of the Cork Opera House. He also acted as Honorary Legal Advisor to countless artistic groups.

As with many of the personalities profiled in this book, Charlie 'found' theatre in the 1940s with Der Breen and the other members of the Presentation College Theatre Guild on the Western Road. He later appeared with the Gilbert and Sullivan Group when he stood in for Maurice McMahon for a matinee performance of *The Pirates of Penzance*. He remembers being terrified at the thought of going on stage; but the man who went on to preside over, chair and drive some momentous changes in Cork's artistic life and to become a highly entertaining after-dinner speaker need not have worried, because he was a 'natural' in the public eye.

The spontaneous warmth of applause which greeted his final appearance after twenty-one years as Chairman of the Cork Film Festival was testament to the respect the citizens have for this cultured gentleman.

Lest we get carried away in our admiration for Charlie, we must step back in time to his *Slag* days. I wondered what really was the reason for their success?

> It was, pure and simply, Colum Fehily's scriptwriting. He was the most clever writer in Ireland. He was even too clever at times, as his brilliance could be missed by his audience, but Michael Twomey and myself made some script changes to bring it down to another level, often to Colum's annoyance. Remember 'slagging' was a new form of wit and humour. We had great fun doing the shows but it was hard work, as we could have as many as thirty costume changes of an evening in the tiny Group Theatre. We had to climb up and down the ladder in the wings for a quick change between sketches.

Charlie agreed that being slagged was seen by some as a form of flattery and, as Donal O'Donovan has said, individuals came to the shows to see if they were actually the subject of the satire.

Charlie's earliest claim to fame was on the rugby and soccer fields. He played rugby for Pres, later earned his colours at UCC and then turned out for Cork Constitution seniors and, when studying in Dublin, for Lansdowne. He played soccer for Western Rovers, and played for University College, Dublin (UCD), though he never attended that university. A playing colleague was the late Brian Lenihan. He lined out for Crosshaven, also in soccer, and played in the Football Association of Ireland Cup for Evergreen when he was just seventeen. An all-rounder, he was on winning Sunday's Well water polo teams and sailed on Cork Harbour waters and beyond.

As a solicitor's apprentice, Charlie was auditor of the Debating Society of Ireland. Honoured for his work for the arts with a Masters from UCC, he has the unique distinction of being elected for two terms to the National College of Art and Design and, in each of his elected terms, serving as chairman for a period of four years. He was also a member of the Arts Council.

Charlie was justifiably proud of ongoing restoration work in the old Royal Yacht Club in Cobh, now the Sirius Arts Centre. The Sirius Trust plans restorative work on this building, which was handed over to it by UCC some forty years ago. The final phase is the building's roof repair, which will be completed when funds are available. In his professional life Charlie introduced his own, completely free, legal aid scheme for those without any means, some years before the Government came up with its system.

Charlie's abiding passion was the Cork Opera House. Executive Director Gerry Barnes, Chairman Charlie, as well as the board and staff, have steered the big theatre through good and bad times. Charlie considered the best future outcome for the Opera House would be ownership of its Trust by Cork City Council; it would mean that those who contributed to the massive fundraising effort from the 1950s through to the mid-1960s (without ever becoming share-holders) would finally be able to say proudly that the Opera House is truly a municipal building.

Niall Toibín with Charlie Hennessy at the English Market
(© Irish Examiner)

Charlie acknowledged the massive support from civil and commercial sources. Per capita the Opera House has a higher seat occupancy rate than any other theatre in Ireland but, because of its size and its comparatively small catchment area, this financial support is a necessity. The theatre now has to pay VAT on returns for touring companies from outside Ireland.

Charlie Hennessy's contribution to Cork's artistic life has indeed been a remarkable achievement and his efforts continue to benefit the theatre-goers of the south. His untimely death in July 2008 created a cultural void in the city that is well nigh impossible to fill.

Chapter 23
Fit-ups and Frost

Vass Anderson

Vass Anderson has done it all. A native of Cork, where he had his first experience of theatre, you are likely to have seen him on countless TV series on BBC and ITV.

In the 1960s Vass left the day job in insurance to find his

Vass Anderson
(© Irish Examiner)

way in London, becoming a respected journalist and earning a precious English Equity card. Vass left Cork, but Cork has always attracted him back whenever he is able to share with old friends the memories of a golden time in Cork theatre.

Vass, Chris Whitnell and Ewan O'Flynn toured the halls of Munster in much the same way as the 'fit-up' companies of old. The tours were mainly in Lent when any other form of public entertainment ('foreign' dances, for instance) was not tolerated by the Church. Each booking included the play and Vass recalls those days with fondness:

> It was early '50s. We did plays like *Rookery Nook* by Ben Travers, or – by another name – *Murder in the Mansion*. We'd follow it up with a comedy item and even a dance, despite the restrictions.
>
> Fellow actor Jim Noonan was by then a veteran of the circuit and played 'dames'; and, just like the fit-ups, we'd drive to a hall, rehearsing in the car on the way. Once, in Tipperary, we got the fright of our lives when the promoter put up our names in lights. We feared that we would not live up to the promotion. Another time our car broke down and we came home in a cattle lorry

Theatre's young bloods were not easily put off. So a company called 'Jet Fenton Presents' was born, the name of which referred to the driving forces, Pat Fenton, now a director of the Opera House, and Jim O'Hanlon, a Dublin comedian. Vass recalls:

> We did a lot of work in the County Cork area. One evening we were short of one cast member and Pat Fenton's wife, then Marion McCarthy, played twins – her own part and then, with a quick costume change, played her sister.
>
> We were going strong. We'd arrive to a hall at eight, but we were lucky if they were ready for us to start by ten o'clock. That was tough, as we were all holding on to our day jobs.

Vass and Frank Duggan worked together in insurance in Cork City. Frank and I did a lot of theatre together. He'd play the piano and write the lyrics. We did a lot of concerts on Sunday nights and our travel limit was Limerick.

In mainstream theatre I was involved with James Stack in the School of Music. He influenced you a lot, and he was very reliable as a director. He'd tell you take four steps over there, turn left, count one and speak. His direction was very tight, but he knew what he was doing, and it always worked. Joe Lynch once said to me in London that he never had to unlearn anything that Stacky taught him. I regarded Stacky as one of the best directors. He wasn't 'method', but instinctively he was fairly close to it. Dan Donovan was very good, but he'd direct more loosely. He gave you a certain amount of leeway.

Vass demonstrated his versatility when he was a member of the Cork Operatic Society.

It [the Society] was desperately short of money so we decided to do a revue. We called it *Operantics* and the writers were Tony Murphy, Michael Twomey, George Crosbie and myself. George wrote a brilliant piece called the 'Bona Fides' and when the relevant law on drink was revoked, I wrote a 'Lament for the Bona Fides'. I also wrote for Mon Murphy about courting practices around the world and also for Siobhán O'Brien. *Operantics* made some money, so we did another, again at the Palace, called *More Operantics*, and it was a big success.

Vass was very much involved with a series of productions at the Father Mathew Hall and says, 'Kevin Breen set up a company with Rex Archer and they did a series of light comedies and also the panto at Christmas in the Father Mathew Hall for which I wrote some topical songs and played the squire and other parts. Each evening David McInerney, Chris Whitnell and myself would perform a topical song, reading from a script in hand. I came on last and had my script, only to find the other two had learned their lines in advance, and so delivered them without an aid. I had to read my lines, and of course the audience thought I hadn't bothered to learn my lines like the other two.'

Theatre was fun for those who were safe in their day jobs in 1960s Ireland, be it Dunlop's, Ford's, insurance, commerce, or whatever. Vass says, 'One man gave up the day job and headed for the UK was Dermot Crowley and he is doing very nicely. We both appeared in an episode of *A Touch of Frost*. He does a lot of radio and on stage appeared in Conor McPherson's *The Weir*.'

For Vass the move to England in the 1960s was forced by circumstance. There were six others in his office, all about the same age and in the same job, and so there was a log-jam with regard to promotion. Vass read an advert about an interview in Dublin for a job in Cork with another insurance office.

I got the job. This was January 1963, and I was in a panto at the same time. But the job did not work out and after six months I left because I was being transferred to Dublin on a reduced salary. Another company was offering a much bigger salary in London. I headed off, took the insurance job there, and got into theatre there through fringe productions. Also I began writing for *Scene* magazine and did a big series on footballers for the *Sunday Independent*. I worked as a freelance and was free to do the bizarre stories. I got my English Equity card because I was now a professional broadcaster. That got me an Irish Equity card, so I began doing voiceovers for RTÉ, working with Spike Milligan, Pauline Delaney, Harry Taub, Anthony Jackson and others. Then *The Irish Post* started and I stayed with them as a freelance for thirty years, writing a column called 'Anderson's People'. I interviewed all the Irish performers including Donal Donnelly, T. P. McKenna, Jim Norton, Ray McNally, Micheál MacLiammóir, Hilton Edwards and Brendan Smith. I do not think there was an Irish performer, actor, singer or dancer that I didn't interview. I wrote for the *Irish Weekly Examiner*, and Crichton Healy on the *Evening Echo* published a lot of my work.

The Bush Theatre opened in 1972. Vass tried unsuccessfully to get a part in one of its productions. Then, just before the opening of *The Relief of Martha King*, an actor fell ill and Vass got the part.

Vass has done quite a bit of film work and actually appeared in the first *Star Wars*, from which came an invitation to attend a Sci-Fi convention in Earls Court. TV work has included: a part in Frank O'Connor's *An Only Child*, with John B.'s brother, Eamon Keane, and shot in Cobh by ITV; *Love Girl* and *The Innocent*, directed by Alan Clarke; and the hit comedy series, *Father Ted*. In all, Vass has appeared in sixty-one plays for TV and sixteen feature films. 'Last year I was in two pop videos for bands I had never heard of: they were Embrace and The Cure. In another promo film, I was supposed to be Graham Norton's hurling coach. It was filmed in Harrow. I appeared in *Murphy's Stroke* and *Pennies from Heaven*.'

Art was imitating life when Vass played the coroner for Cork in *Follow the Dream*. It had an all-star cast, including Claire Bloom and Deborah Kerr. There was a scene in court that supposedly took place in Cork and the City Coroner was presiding. 'I said I'd love to play the part, as my grandfather and uncle (James and Joseph McCabe) were both City Coroners. I got it and it was shot in a Hammersmith courthouse. When I look at my time in insurance in Cork, the thought then of appearing on TV would be like walking on the moon. And yet, I have worked with Marlon Brando, Alec Guinness and became a very good friend of Cyril Cusack before his death.'

Vass loved his work for the Cork Film Festival. 'I'd organise Festival events in London. I worked on the visit to Cork of Peter Gilmore, then the star of the TV series *The Onedin Line*. I also brought to Cork Simon Williams, Jean Anderson, Edward Woodward, Honor Blackman, Judy Geeson and many others, and I acted as their official escort at the request of Dermot Breen.'

In his early days Vass decided to put something back into the area where he had lived in London and had taught drama to children. Because of this he moved to other drama study work and then joined the teaching staff of the London Academy (of media, films and TV) where he worked for twenty years. 'Anytime I needed time off to do other things, because they were professionals themselves, I got the time to pursue my acting and writing careers.'

Married in London, it has indeed been a long and interesting road for Vass. His twice-yearly visits to Cork keep him in touch with a city and its people which he obviously loves so much.

Chapter 24
Theatre by Design

Jim Queally

The name Jim Queally might not immediately ring a bell with lovers of great comedy, but the man has made an enormous contribution to the performing arts in his adopted Cork.

TV viewers might know him first and best for his portrayal of Theo Wigmore in *Killinaskully*. Theo, a cultured, debonair, somewhat toffee-nosed individual, contrasts admirably with the nefarious and hilarious characters fleshed out by Pat Shortt.

Theo is simply the latest in a myriad of roles brought to life on stage and camera by the talented Mr Queally. It has been a long and winding road from Wickham Street, in the heart of Limerick City, to the suburb of Blackrock in Cork where Jim now resides. The story of his journey makes for fascinating reading.

Born in May 1939 – 'just as Hitler was thinking of going into Poland' – Jim remembers being brought by his father to see the seaplanes at Foynes. He considers the establishment of Rineanna – now Shannon Airport – as a turning point in the fortunes of Limerick.

Not unlike the earlier seminal memory of the Limerick of Frank McCourt, Jim recalls the poverty of the city, but his obvious love of that time and place, his somewhat cosseted up-bringing, still warm his thoughts of home.

Jim Queally came easily to the stage.

When I was about ten years old, my mother brought me to see a production by the fit-up company, the McFaddens, but my first real introduction to theatre came through the College Players in Limerick in 1956. St Munchin's College gave the Players the use of their theatre, hence the name. By the time I joined them they had moved to their own premises in Theatre Lane. On that lane was the stage door of the Theatre Royal which fronted on to Henry Street and was burned down in the '20s.

Our theatre seated 200. It was situated in what was once a Georgian garden with the entrance in the lane and the stage door in O'Connell Street. We were a bit like the old Everyman Playhouse in Cork, in that we were an amateur company with professional standards. Our seasons ran from August to the following April on a two weekly rep basis. We ran from Sunday to Sunday, performing nightly; and at the same time we would rehearse for the next production.

By day I was doing the bookings and looking after the little theatre. We operated on a 'share basis', so by the age of sixteen I was earning a living from theatre. On each final Sunday night, there would be a 'treasury call'. Cast assembled on the stage, all the accounts were declared: what the play had cost, what they had taken at the box office, what the profit was and what the share of that profit was for individual cast members. You were given your money there and then. It was all very open and honest.

I had gone to Limerick Art School and I designed my first set for the Players when I was seventeen. It was for the play *My Three Angels*.

A youthful Jim Queally as Willie Shanahan in Early And Often *from the College Players, Limerick in 1958*
(© Michael Martin)

The somewhat idyllic theatre life was to be shattered for the Players and Jim when the theatre burned down in 1959. It was a huge blow. The company was now without a home. That year, the famous Todd's store also burned down, a double blow to the artistic and commercial life of the city. The College Players would battle on, but not at the same pace or with the same output.

Chance can be a fine thing in all our lives. Jim was involved in a production of Lennox Robinson's *Church Street*. In the cast was Corkman Dave Coughlan, brother of actor, Dan. Dave was working in personnel in Shannon. He told Jim about the first plans to present medieval banquets in Bunratty Castle. He set up a meeting between Jim and the quite remarkable Brendan O'Regan, the man who drove Shannon Development to such heights and was the prime mover in the cross-border Cooperation North.

Others present at that meeting were Brendan's secretary, Kitty O'Connor, and Ruth Hill, display manager at the Shannon Free shop. Also present was South African John Garde who had been a submarine commander in the war and was involved in the hotel business. These were just a few of the people who were in at the very beginning of the medieval banquets which thrive to this day at Bunratty and other venues in the region.

> It had all begun on an experimental basis. John Garde and myself had a small office on the periphery of the airport, and there we recruited the very first Bunratty Singers. Kitty O'Connor wrote the first scripts and rehearsed wonderful 'medieval' songs . . . by Percy French! I went to Dublin to pick out the first costumes from Gings. I was the first actor to welcome patrons from the minstrel's gallery in Bunratty Castle on a summer's evening in 1962.
>
> I stayed with it for twelve months and then headed off to the Phoenix Theatre in Leicester and was there a few years.

Jim made the Cork connection when he became display manager at the Queen's Old Castle store in 1964.

'However, I was made redundant in 1968 and I had to earn my living from the theatre, plus a bit of freelance display work, until 1969 when I was asked to return to Bunratty. I worked in not only Bunratty, but also in the Folk Park, Dunguaire and Knappogue Castles. Those five years were incredible as anybody who was anybody seemed to pass through the castles.'

One evening stands out for Jim. He received a request after the show to go to a private party and do his *seanachaí* act for a mysterious visitor and friends at Dromoland Castle. It was a select group of about a dozen people celebrating a birthday.

I was introduced to the 'birthday boy' who happened to be Bob Hope. I don't suffer from nerves but I was concerned, as he sat only a few feet from me. I only had two stories. After the first he applauded and laughed and shook my hand and pleaded for the second in my repertoire of two. I did that and he came over and hugged me and said: 'You remind me so much of my times with Barry Fitzgerald. He'd tell all those stories from Ireland, very few of which I believed, but they were all very funny.'

I did not have the courage to ask him for his autograph. It was a privilege to perform for someone as iconic as that. I also performed for Richard Nixon. He gave me a present of a tie-pin which was later stolen.

It was a wonderful time, myself and my family lived in Shannon, but after five years I began to wonder where was it leading to. Money was good but you 'age out' of tights. I was in my thirties, married with two children.

Chance again intervened. Jim noticed an *Examiner* page that had fallen open on the kitchen floor and an advert caught his eye. It stated that a display manager was required in Cashs of Cork. 'I drove to Cork and got the job at £4,000 a year, which was big money then. I was there for about eight years,' he says.

Jim had worked with Everyman when they were in the CCYMS Theatre in Castle Street. Outstanding theatre man Donn McMullin was general manager there in those days and they became firm friends.

One of Jim's happiest memories was working with Limerick comedy duo Tom and Pascal. He has vivid recall of travelling up from his native city in 1964 with the lads, props in the back seat, as he sought to grapple with his role as feed guy in one of their incredibly successful nights before adoring Cork audiences at the Father Mathew Hall.

> I played Horatio to Michael Twomey's Hamlet and in my time I must have appeared in over twelve pantos under the direction of Michael at the Opera House. I loved traditional panto and I was usually the Baron who married the dame at the end.
>
> I was also in the first panto which broke with all that great tradition and did not enjoy the experience in Christmas 2000.
>
> I did a lot of radio, including a comedy series called *Natural Gas*. Featured were Michael Twomey, Frank Duggan, James N. Healy and guests such as Billa O'Connell, Dave McInerney and Paddy Comerford.

Jim's first experience of TV was work done for *Hall's Pictorial Weekly* with Michael Twomey, Frank Duggan and Biddy McGrath from Limerick.

We were in Tralee to do a sort of satirical programme filmed in the courthouse. TV came late to me and it is still a learning curve. It is more difficult than theatre. You have to learn to pull back, to learn the disciplines that are imposed by the technical restraints. It has the advantage that once it is done, that's it.

I appeared in feature films – *Broken Harvest, The Aristocrats* and *Falling for a Dancer* – and for TV, in *St Oscar* for London Weekend Television: and I appeared in a couple of episodes of *Fair City*. I did a little film called *Razor Fish* with Brenda Fricker in west Cork.

A phone call led to Jim's appearing in *Killinaskully*. It was from Mike Finn, the writer. Jim had worked with him for Island Theatre Company in Limerick. Killoskully, near Newport, is where 'Jacksie's' pub is located. The interior shots were filmed there and the outside scenes were done in Ballinahinch.

I asked Jim why he thought *Killinaskully* was so popular, since it consistently tops the ratings. 'It seems to span age groups. Small children love it. Apparently it is not watched much within the Pale – or at least they tend not to admit to watching it! But it certainly is loved in the rest of the country. It is probably the most successful situation comedy series that RTÉ have done.'

I wondered if Jim still preferred theatre. 'The older I get the more I want to design for theatre rather than perform.' (He came up with a wonderfully authentic sets for *Private Lives* (2008) and *An Inspector Calls* (2007) at the Everyman Palace.)

'I love TV and I love the sense of fun involved in working on *Killinaskully*. Pat Shortt not only plays all those parts but is one of the writers. He is very likeable and professional to work with. *Killinaskully* has given a lot of employment to a lot of actors, some of us on a regular basis. We film from early April to the beginning of July and then there are three months of editing before the series is shown in September and October. We work to a very tight schedule.'

Looking back now on a crowded and successfully varied career in the performance arts and theatre design, Jim has particularly fond memories of James N. Healy.

I have a distinct memory of meeting this man with a gingery beard in the bar of the Group Theatre in South Main Street. Someone said to me that it was James N. I had heard an awful lot about him and knew he was an icon in the Group Theatre which he had founded. The Southern Theatre group were based there. I hardly spoke to him that night and I considered him perhaps a bit austere, a bit distant, but between then, which was about 1966, and up to his death in 1993, we became incredibly close friends. Hardly a week

James N. Healy researching another show at his house on Grattan Hill in October 1987
(© Donal O'Donovan)

went by in the 1980s and 1990s that I did not go up to his house on Grattan Hill. We'd have tea in his front room upstairs. It was there and on our journeys to various productions that I developed a warm affection and respect for James N.

I asked about James N.'s strengths.

It was his art of characterisation. His portrayal of the matchmaker in *Sive* could never be surpassed. I don't believe any other actor could quite capture the essence of that character as Jim did. Within the matchmaker there is a great isolation and loneliness. The marriages he made for other people, he could not manage to make for himself.

I found the matchmaker a fascinating character, as I was in productions of *Sive* time and time again with Jim in the '60s and early '70s. I was the young lover. He was supposed to be about nineteen and I was twenty-seven when I played it first. It was revived so often and James once asked me to do it again, but I was then forty. 'You can dye your hair and you'll be grand,' James said. We toured the country with *Sive*. We'd meet at the Group Theatre, have our sandwiches, and then off to Limerick or somewhere else, always returning to Cork after the show.

James N. created a whole evening on Percy French and wrote a book based on French's songs and poems. He brought that show to America and lectured on French. His book on castles is a wonderfully interesting book.

That whole era of the Southern Theatre Group was a remarkably exciting time.

It must be remembered that during that time in Ireland there was no 'quality theatre' on tour. The Abbey did not tour or, if they did, it would only be to one or two selected venues. The first company to be set up specifically to go on tour was the Irish Theatre Company and that didn't survive very long. Touring then was neglected in this country and James N. was rectifying that situation. We toured Munster and did only a limited season in Dublin because most of the cast had jobs in Cork and could only perform in holiday time.

Jim Queally as Jamesie in Silver Wedding *from Theatre Of The South at the Opera House*

James N. left Ford's and joined Eustace's, but when that failed he had to make a living from his theatre work.

While I was another generation, I could see in his talents as a performer, and in his sense of design, that James N. was very much a fellow traveller. I learned from him. There was a great wisdom in him. If you needed advice, you could go to James N. I had no idea on that first brief meeting in the Group theatre bar that we would become such good friends. I missed him so much when he died and I still do. He was a huge loss to the theatre community in Cork and to the very tapestry of theatre in the city. He was a colourful character but, much more than that, he was a great human being.

I wondered if Jim had worked with James N. on any of his Gilbert and Sullivan productions?

I designed the set for his final *Mikado* in the Auditorium in the old Cork School of Music. I was glad I did that, and I also have the immense satisfaction that I was in the last play that James N. ever attended. The company was Playground and we did *Gaslight* which James N. came to see. We then did *Groping for Words* and I remember we had a photo-call on the very day James N. was buried.

His contribution was truly immense and perhaps not as appreciated as much as it should have been. It is rather heartbreaking to-day to work with young

Fashion Statement by Jim Queally in Killinaskully

actors to whom the name James N. Healy means nothing. But then I have worked with young people in Druid who had come from the acting school but had never heard of MacLiammóir or Hilton Edwards. You'd wonder why in their training they are not taught the history of theatre in this country.

I asked Jim what were his favourite roles.

One would be in *Waiting for Godot*, as the more cheerful Estragon. That was with the Cork Theatre Company. I found Beckett to be a bit like cricket, in that it tends to be a participant sport. We rehearsed for almost six weeks and we got into Beckett's mind a bit. We really knew what the play was about but the audience did not have that luxury of six weeks. For all that, we did very well, running for over a month. That was in the old Ivernia Theatre, off Grand Parade. My other favourite would be as Thornton Wilder's stage-manager in *Our Town*, for Island Theatre. I loved, too, being Max in *Sound of Music*, and Colonel Pickering in *My Fair Lady*, with Michael Twomey – a superb Professor Higgins.

Just a few weeks after I spoke to Jim came the tragic news that his only son, Ian, had died. It was borne by Jim with great dignity and public calm, as he drew deeply on his Christian faith and the promise of life eternal.

Chapter 25
The Art of Farce

Frank Fitzgerald

Now retired from service with the Met in Shannon and Cork, Frank Fitzgerald was an Everyman stalwart with a great sense of design – in fact his stage designs for the group are remembered favourably to this day. He has interesting views to share on the subject of comedy in general, and farce in particular.

Comedians make people laugh, but comedy is not as easily defined. Of course, with some it may induce loud laughter, while with others only the odd chuckle. At one extreme, it may just bring smiles of contented pleasure, while at the other, gasps of strangled laughter as situations of pure farce overtake one another.

In the theatre some comic situations occur on the night though not in the script. One of these that I recall involved a door. Doors in stage sets normally open 'on stage' but occasionally open 'off', because of the relationship between scenes and the outer rooms or spaces. Again, the doors normally open upstage and only very rarely do they open down, when a special effect is demanded. To counter any possible errors in this regard, stage-managers tend to block incorrect openings and to place very clear directions off-stage. One night an actor was slightly late with his entrance and pushed a door 'on'. It jammed at the floor, but the actor continued to push higher up. He then proceeded to climb through the v-shaped opening, accompanied by gales of laughter from the audience. A moment of pure, but unintended farce!

A Scent of Flowers, by James Saunders, was staged by Everyman in the Little Theatre, Castle Street. It was a tragic story of the suicide of a vulnerable girl called Zoe, played by Heather Underwood – certainly not a comedy. However, it did produce two comic situations outside the theatre.

One scene required two wooden trestles for the support of the coffin. I made these at home and painted them black, and left them to dry in our kitchen. A superstitious decorator was far from comfortable next day, when he found that he had to work 'around' them.

The coffin for the scene was borrowed from Cash's workshop in Caroline Street. After the play closed it had to be returned on the following Monday morning. It was reasonably light, so I placed it on a roof-rack atop my old Ford Prefect. Traffic was fairly heavy in Patrick Street that morning and came to a stop several times, much to the amusement of some of the onlookers, though some blessed themselves and prayed for the poor soul that was being carried in the coffin. Surely no one deserved the indignity of being carried on top of an old Prefect!

Frank recalls productions by Cork Youth Theatre. The aspirants were introduced to the practicalities of stage work when they presented *Spreading the News* by Lady Gregory and *The Knacker's ABC* at Everyman.

Amongst those associated with those emerging talents in young Everyman was one Fifi Wilson, later to become internationally known as Fiona Shaw. Another farce from Lady Gregory's time is *The Tinker's Wedding* by J. M. Synge. It was presented, about 1970, as *Pósadh an Tincéara*.

Farce is largely based on absurd situations carried by rapid and confusing movement. These were very evident in the Everyman production of Feydeau's *Hotel Paradiso*. In contrast to that, physical movement in *Theatre of the Absurd* slows often to the static,

Frank Fitzgerald's twisted tree suggesting Calvary with brooding cyclorama Noel Murphy and Pat Butler in Waiting For Godot, *Everyman 1968–69 Season at The Little Theatre, Castle Street.*

yet there is much that is farcical in what is presented. One thinks of *Waiting for Godot* or *Happy Days*. Farce and the absurd were to be found, too, in a wonderful play by Tom Stoppard called *Rosencrantz and Guildenstern Are Dead*.

Over the years Everyman hosted many productions from other companies. The *Happy Days* production featured O. Z. Whitehead. Then there was an outstanding presentation of Dylan Thomas's *Under Milkwood*, featuring Brian de Salvo. I designed the set for Peter O'Shaughnessy's production with Theatre of the South, another Feydeau comedy–farce, *The Gamecock*.

Frank Fitzgerald – a designer working within a tight budget – represents all that is commendable in the efforts of so many people in semi-professional and amateur theatre who give their time, energy and genius to so many companies without ever having their names in lights.

Somebody once said to me that when the lights go down and the curtain opens, theatre is in the hands of the stage-manager and his or her crew until the lights come up again in the auditorium. Let's hear it then for the designers, lighting, sound and backstage people on whom a production rises or falls.

Chapter 26
Smitten by Panto

Jim Mulcahy

We never know when we are being influenced for the good. Sometimes we unwittingly receive a blueprint, a kind of map, or even a sort of jigsaw, for what is to be our future. We may not even recognise it. It can shape our thinking and prompt us to move in a direction that we might not otherwise have taken – a direction that we might have missed, but which brings something that becomes central to our lives in years to come.

Blackpool boy Jim Mulcahy went to North Monastery Primary and encountered Denis Harrington, teacher and respected member of the then thriving Cork theatre community. Teacher Denis was very much associated with Cork comedy theatre, but he was known nationally for his work on Din Joe Fitzgibbon's *Take the Floor*, which was compulsive listening on Radio Éireann. It was claimed that *Take the Floor* was the only radio show on which you could hear, not see, Irish dancing.

It must be remembered that radio was then at the centre of household entertainment. It was the central attraction in any living-room, much as TV is now. Families gathered in a house to listen to their favourite programmes, invariably on Radio Éireann. Those programmes included *Take the Floor* and *Balladmaker's Saturday Night,* one of whose stars was another famous Corkman, Joe Lynch.

Denis Harrington was a prime mover in the CCYMS Hall and the general Cork panto scene. More importantly for Jim Mulcahy, he was teacher in fourth class where Jim was a shy pupil.

> I was in awe of him and he was a very funny man in class. I'd go to see him in panto, and say to myself, 'I'd love to do that.' Then one day he came into class: 'Mulcahy, I think you'd be very good on stage. He persuaded me to join the large cast in a play about the burning of Cork. I loved the whole experience.
>
> My parents brought me to the pantos at Christmas. At the time there were twelve productions in and around Cork and I got to see them all with my mother, Bina. We'd even go out of the city to Coachford and Fermoy. My idols were Paddy Comerford and Billa. I'd catch Barrett and Sullivan in the Sunday night concert series in the Glen Hall. Some of my pals could not understand my growing interest in theatre. I loved solo singing and I joined Collins Musical Society. I was in the chorus for *Rose Marie* in the Opera House.

The Vagabond King followed and then *Show Boat* came along.

Liam Smith, of Haulbowline Theatre fame, was directing *Show Boat* and one night at rehearsals he asked Jim to read the part of Frank. 'He saw me panic and told me to be myself and read the lines. The next morning I got a call at my workplace in Harrington Goodlass Wall to be at rehearsal that night. That evening I sang for musical director, Bunny Kealy, and was told that I was Frank. Playing opposite me was Aileen Cooney, an established artiste, as Ellie. Liam Smith told me to go out and enjoy myself and I did. I was just eighteen.'

Jim was beside himself with nerves and did not eat for a week, but the opening night came on 10 March 1975 and the show was a hit. Jim was hooked. 'It was a great time for me. Dan Coughlan was a truly great comedy actor. He was fabulous as Cap'n Andy. He had previously played the role of Frank, so he gave me an awful lot of advice. In that show Joe Stockdale was Rubberface, and we've been great friends ever since. Those weeks in the Opera House built my confidence. I was never afraid of a role after that.'

When Collins ended its glorious chapter in the cultural and artistic life of the city, many of the society's members moved to the Cork Operatic Society where a production of *The Desert Song* introduced Jim to his future wife, Marion Healy, who was in the chorus. It was love from the start.

Another show, *Gypsy Love*, was Jim's introduction to Catherine Mahon Buckley of Cork Academy of Dramatic Art. 'We played lovers in *Gypsy Love* and Catherine asked if I'd get involved with other shows. She was producing O'Casey's *Plough and the Stars*, and I agreed to do the stage management. To my amazement, I was nominated for the Drama Critics Award and won it.'

Catherine was planning to stage the panto at the Everyman

Step aside, I'm coming through: Eoin Hally and Jim Mulcahy in a scene from Jack And The Beanstalk *at the Palace*

(© Everyman Palace Ltd)

Palace. Previously, Donie Gleeson had produced a panto in the Lough Hall. Terrific tenor Maurice O'Donovan told Jim that he was to play the dame and did not give him an option. 'As it turned out, I always wanted to play the dame, so I agreed. Paddy Coughlan of the *Swans* did the set. For me the two greatest dames were Paddy himself and Paddy Cotter.'

After the Lough panto, Paddy Coughlan presented Jim with the apron used by Paddy in the *Swans* shows. It was recognition for Jim that he was now accepted into the 'Panto Dame Academy'. Paddy told him he was the nearest thing to the way he had played the dame, which was praise indeed.

'Catherine's first panto in the Everyman Palace was *Cinderella* in 1992. I played one of the Ugly Sisters with Paul Dennehy, who also wrote the script. Another year, in *Sleeping Beauty*, Paul was the dame and I was the king. I've been mother to Robinson Crusoe and Red Riding Hood's granny, but my favourite role of all is the dame.'

Jim has appeared in some fourteen pantos at the Everyman Palace and he has made some very dramatic entrances: on a motor bike, a golf buggy – once he was even catapulted on to the stage from the wings. It was suggested one year that he would fly in from the balcony. Riggers had a huge sling ready, but Jim mentioned a bad back and that was that.

I spoke with Jim on a beautiful June day, but, like the toy manufacturers, Catherine and Jim were ahead of the game, thinking about Christmas and the panto *Red Riding Hood* for 2008–2009. That, as they say, is showbiz!

Chapter 27
Spitting Image

Pakie O'Callaghan

I was speaking to Pakie O'Callaghan on the day after Bertie Ahern took his leave of the Dáil. Watching it on TV it had struck me that we are, to put it mildly, a most contradictory race. Those same people who hitherto had not a good word for him in the Dáil were now, for the most part, suggesting that the country had lost a great leader. His erstwhile critics would no doubt say that this is the very stuff of politics; nothing is to be taken as personal.

Pakie, who has that remarkable 'ear' for the famous, must have felt that he was losing a 'friend', as his uncannily accurate impersonation of the then Taoiseach had entertained radio listeners on the *Joe Duffy Show* and elsewhere in the weeks prior to his resignation.

That is, if you like, another cruel twist for those in public life. Once you step out of the limelight, you are taken off the shelves of public interest and the focus is on the next incumbent of a high office. Pakie admitted that he was already grappling with the earthy vowel sounds of Offaly's famous son, Brian Cowen.

I have spent the last two weeks trying to get a handle on Cowen's voice. He had emerged, not unexpectedly, but more rapidly than it was first thought he would. The reality for me was that 'Claraman' was now the new kid on the block and if I couldn't catch the voice then I'm out of the game.

I have a *modus operandi*, which I'm not going to reveal, as it's a sort of trade secret, but I apply the normal methodology when I'm attempting to get a voice. A lot of voices I have never succeeded in getting. I try to identify an idiosyncrasy. For An Taoiseach, there is the elongated vowel sound and this is followed by a rush over the apparently inconsequential part of the sentence. Then it is back into the substance of what he wanted to say.

Charlie McCreevey was the main guy, but when he went to Europe my whole act, the after-dinner turn, just disappeared. Once he went away, I did not do him again. It was the same with the late Charlie Haughey. Dessie O'Malley was my first. I began in the late '70s in a very small way with Dessie and Brian Farrell of RTÉ. I was doing Pádraig Flynn for almost twenty years. He was always relevant right into the '90s. For impact these personalities need to be on the front page, not on page six of our newspapers. So Bertie is now gone as far as my act is concerned.

I wondered where this sense of mimicry came from. Its origins were not at all dramatic.

> I came from a very large extended family. My mother's father was a market gardener in the area and he gave the family the land, so herself and her brothers and sisters, when they married, lived in an unbroken row of seven houses on the Glasheen Road in Cork. The result was that I had twenty-nine first cousins, all in a row. They would not all have been my contemporaries, but there was always a ready-made audience. It was a fun-filled time for me, growing up in the '50s and '60s, as I'd visit those other houses.
>
> A lot of my own cousins are very good mimics; we'd be taking off each other within the families. Our subjects were usually from within the family group and we kept it amongst ourselves, rather than doing it at parties outside the family circle.
>
> My mother's family were from the original heart of Cork in Pouladuff, but most of them married people from the country, so they were a very eclectic grouping. My own father was from Schull. The first time I ever went public was in the company of friends on the way to a match in the old Athletic Grounds, when I took off RTÉ's Bill O'Herlihy, who at the time was a reporter with *Seven Days*. It developed from there. The first ever paid gig was from a firm of accountants, Stokes Kennedy Crowley, at Arbutus Lodge Hotel. I got sixty old pounds for it, which was more than two weeks' wages at the time.

I recall seeing Pakie in an excellent production of *Who's Afraid of Virginia Woolf*, with Ann Dorgan, Nuala Casey and Ber Power, and direction by Michael Twomey.

> I was quite active at the time in Everyman Extra with Michael McGrath, Frank Fitzgerald, Pat Talbot, and a youth initiator Emelie FitzGibbon who went on to found the excellent theatre in education company Graffitti and for whom I had tremendous admiration. I was in my early twenties, so I was helping out and appearing in small-scale productions. There was a period when I was very active. In the late '70s, I was busy with the day jobs in Casey's, auctioneering with Keane Mahony Smith, and then, later again, in commercial cleaning. I felt a little that I was the odd one out in a bohemian world of theatre. I loved being around the theatre scene and it still appeals to me. I like the people in theatre – I find them endearing.

> I was involved with Cork Theatre Company with Ger FitzGibbon and Gerry Barnes, doing three or four plays a year at the old Ivernia Theatre on the Grand Parade. Then I gave up theatre completely for fifteen years. I had heavy family and work commitments and lost interest.

> In 1997 the economy had really taken off. It was difficult to get staff. I was doing a sixty-hour week, so great was the demand for our commercial cleaning services. One Sunday afternoon I was in Penrose Quay picking up polystyrene balls from under the wheel of a car . . . [the cleaning company was clearing up litter after the removal of a computer firm].

I asked myself if this was what I wanted to do with my life. There and then I rang Alf McCarthy. He had been doing a programme with Alan Shortt and Frank Twomey called *Shortt Circuit*. They were doing a range of characters . . . [not including] Charlie McCreevey. I also felt that my Brian Farrell could act as the anchorman in their excellent sketches. I'd be McCreevey, Farrell and Charlie Bird, with appearances by my Dessie O'Malley. I also loved being P. Flynn. It went out on Saturday mornings. It was a sort of successor to *Scrap Saturday*. Alf, as producer, took me on board, so I'd go into the Cork studios two days a week and write sketches.

I wrote one, which was known as *A Reading From the Book of Deseronomy*. It was a kind of commentary on political events of the previous week. After ten weeks on the show, I received a phone call from RTÉ producer John Keogh.

At the time of the call, Pakie was indulging his passion for hillwalking. He and a few pals were tracing their steps along the border, having been inspired by a Colm Tóibín book. John asked Pakie on the phone if he was Pakie O'Callagahan the comedian. Pakie said 'no', and meant it. It took another call before they made contact and Pakie found himself in the studios at Donnybrook.

I found a complete air of unreality about the whole affair. I had not gone to drama school, I was not an actor. I was to do my take of Charlie McCreevey in the new show. I walked into Studio 4 and found it hard to take it all in. We made a pilot show of what was to become *Bull Island*, one of the most popular home-produced TV comedy shows ever to come out of RTÉ.

Alan Shortt was Bertie, Frank Twomey was Celia, and I was Charlie McCreevey. It achieved top ratings and lasted for three years. We'd do nine programmes in the spring and another nine in the autumn.

Pakie was able to keep the day job going with the help of his sister and supervisors.

I'd head off for Dublin and Montrose on Monday mornings. We'd write it Monday and Tuesday, and then Wednesday and Thursday we'd film it. Because of my appearances on TV each week, I'd often have a choice of three gigs on a Friday or a Saturday. I was staying with my auntie in Drumcondra. I was able to see three or four plays a week when I was up recording *Bull Island*. It was fantastic. Those were three great years and I enjoyed myself. I was very lucky that my wife and then growing family were so supportive. I know that I've been lucky to have been able to do something which gave me so much pleasure. I wrote one script which drew from the infamous Senator McCarthy trials in the States. That was the only one that I can remember which upset the Government. I did feel that many of the other scripts were not sharp enough.

Interestingly Pakie is not a fan of TV and admits to never

having watched *Spitting Image* or other political satire shows. 'I was asked once to do a sketch with a Del Boy [David Jason] character in it and I told them that I had never seen the series.'

Charlie McCreevey and Pakie never actually met. A few times they'd both be in Montrose with Pakie rehearsing *Bull Island* and Charlie coming in for a *Prime Time*. It was suggested that Pakie might like to meet the

Man of many voices Pakie O'Callaghan

Finance Minister, but Pakie felt that it was better if he did not, preferring to keep his artistic distance. On another occasion Charlie's office rang to invite Pakie to a photo opportunity with Charlie and himself holding up the Budget disc, but again Pakie declined.

However, they did speak to each other on the phone once. When Pakie was celebrating his fiftieth birthday at home with family and friends, a mutual friend, Pat Harty from Naas, arranged for Charlie to ring and wish Pakie a happy birthday. Pat had hoped to connect up a whole set of speakers to broadcast the conversation between the real Charlie and his imitator around the house, but a power failure ruled that out.

Charlie wished Pakie well; Pakie replied that, whoever it was on the phone, he was a very poor imitation of McCreevey. The real Charlie thanked Pakie for all he had done – no doubt the man from the short grass county was aware that imitation is the purest form of flattery. Pakie says he has always admired Charlie for his self-confidence and the way in which he handled the TV representation of him in his role as Minister for Finance.

Pakie worked for a brief spell on the Vincent Brown TV show, *Midnight Court*. Pakie was to write two sketches a week – they would be filmed on Sunday afternoon and slotted into the live show on RTÉ that night. 'I enjoyed it, as I'm a bit of a political 'anorak', so I wrote scripts on the Nice Treaty and I loved to take off Garrett FitzGerald.'

However, the format was changed and Pakie felt that it did not work, so Pakie just made two appearances. 'I then wrote a stage show, *In the National Interest*, opening in the Opera House with a subsequent tour to seventeen venues around the country.'

From the corridors of power to the club scene in Santa Ponsa is a quantum leap. Pakie took the challenge with another refugee from *Bull Island*, the brilliant Frank Twomey. *Santa Ponsa* is a visually funny stage show which has two Cork 'ladies' in pursuit of sun, sea and sangria, with murderous Mafia figures in the background and two husbands who find themselves in a Spanish jail. It was a far cry from *Virginia Woolf* or the Leinster House bar for Pakie and Frank, but it has had two successful runs at the Everyman Palace, followed by a tour.

Pakie's latest work is another one-man show. He is a *seanachaí* figure, commentating on contemporary Ireland. His pal Charlie is in Brussels. Pakie misses him, we all do. Perhaps he'll drop in when Pakie is back on stage where he belongs.

Chapter 28
Bosco and Bull

Frank Twomey

Mary O'Rourke and Celia Larkin might be interested to know that Bull Islander Frank Twomey did not exactly hit the boards running. He 'stumbled' onto a stage at the ripe old age of thirteen. I let Frank tell me the story in his own words.

> I was at school at the Mon and I joined the Gerald Griffin Youth Club Drama Group. I was very much working backstage and took no part in rehearsals. I was, however, a very good mimic of my teachers and others.
>
> One day there was the absence of a cast member due to a family commitment. I was literally hauled in to the Group Theatre in South Main Street for that night's performance. I think it was a pantomime. It could have been a version of *Red Riding Hood*. I spent the night ad libbing.

That was my first taste of the stage and I was hooked. I had found something that I was good at. I wanted to perform. I imagine it is the thing that drives people in sport, like Seán Óg Ó hAilpín. We see them on All-Ireland or other big match days, but we have no idea that for four nights of the week they are sweating blood in training.

I was a typically bored teenager and now I had found something that I was interested in. I was willing to go out of my way to get to rehearsals. I found a form of expression of myself. There was nothing we couldn't do, there was song, choral verse and dance, drama; there was no specialising. I became involved in Penny Youth Theatre with John Roche. It was a kind of *Tops of the Town* School of Acting. You learned by doing or, more to the point, you learned by *not* doing. It was not the Gaiety School of Acting. It was not academic. We did it all.

Out of school Frank joined the ranks of the real employed. In his early twenties he had a job but the evenings were for theatre. This was his part-time job.

I was forever in plays. I was a sales rep by day, and that night I'd be in the theatre. I worked out of Cork, much my own boss, and had an office in Dunlop House, a company car, good money and happy enough with both. Trouble was I was not really a business person. I wasn't motivated about figures, whether they were up or down. I wanted more and more to be on the stage.

I was a very experienced performer with the Montfort group and they were looked up to in Cork. We were doing *West Side Story*. I have no idea why, but producer Noel Pearson was in the house. He saw it, and offered me a part in his production of *One Flew Over the Cuckoo's Nest*. But to take the role I had to give up the day job. I saw my boss in Dublin and told him I wanted to be an actor. They were very good – they left me keep the company car for a month.

My mind was made up. I did *Cuckoo* with Ray McNally, Liam Neeson and John Kavanagh, with a brilliant Joan O'Hara as Nurse Ratchett. I saw McNally at work every night and he was only magic. That was a stunning production. In 1980 I moved to Dublin to do *Oliver!*, with Noel Pearson again producing. I did *Many Young Men of Twenty* with Joe Lynch. I was the TD's son. Joe Lynch was Danger Mulally and Marie Conmee was Kitty Curley.

I was versatile, so it became a week's work here, and a week's work there. I had a part-time job for survival and then I was acting in the evening when I could get it.

The break every actor is looking for came to Frank in 1983. It came from an unexpected source, gift-wrapped in a box. Frank had got into children's programming in RTÉ. He had done a succession of auditions, but was not right for any of the roles on offer; and then Paula Lambert and the Lambert Puppet Theatre presented Irish TV with its most popular character to date, Bosco.

I met Paula before the audition and there was a working chemistry between us from the beginning. Paula was the voice of Bosco and Marion Richardson was the other presenter. We did a pilot 'dummy' show and if I had known that the day before, I would not have turned up. I knew nothing about TV. We did it and I had not a glimmer that I would get it – I was so laid back, it came across that I was being natural; but in fact I had so little idea as to how I should do it that I was just myself. It proved to be very good television for kids and it became hugely successful.

Bosco kept Frank afloat in Dublin for seven years with repeats. There was a *Bosco* made for nine months of each year.

The problem was that when it ended, Frank Twomey was known only to the public as the presenter of *Bosco*. The dreaded curse for every actor, typecasting, had set in.

There was a price for my being with *Bosco* for so long. I'd go for auditions, but I'd be told that I could not be used as the ad could be for pints of stout and I'd be recognised as the face of *Bosco*. Typecasting drove me out of Dublin. I had run out of road and roles.

I moved back to Cork and was doing odds and ends in RTÉ Cork and on the stage, including stand-up comedian. I was the MC in Gorby's Night Club for nearly two years. I loved it. I did the production side of children's programmes. I did a few pantos and picked up a Best Supporting Actor Award in a Corcadorca production of *Talbot's Box*, with direction

by Pat Kiernan. I had come home to Cork with holes
in my shoes and now it was happening for me again.

Conall Creedon, he of the talented Creedons (including John,
Blake and Norah), was writing a sort of radio soap, *Under the
Goldie Fish*, which was to prove phenomenally successful with
Cork local radio audiences.

That was a time when RTÉ were doing what they once did
best and should never have ceased to do, ensuring that the Cork
public had its own local radio station. Frank joined the cast that
included Alan Shortt, Conor Tallon, Kay Ray Malone, Peter
O'Mahony, Paddy Dunlea, and others, with Aidan Stanley
producing. It ran daily for ten minutes and there was an
omnibus on Sundays, broadcast on the national network.

'That led to the radio show, *Shortt Circuit*, with Alan,
directed by Alf McCarthy. I loved that show and they were my
favourite days. The political satire was good. I was Mary
O'Rourke, David Norris and David Hanley. That then led to
the televised version of *Shortt Circuit*, which was *Bull Island*. It
ran for three years.'

Frank was Mary O'Rourke and Celia Larkin, in the
somewhat confined corridors of power, mingling with other
notables such as Willie O'Dea, David Trimble, Senator Norris,
Charlie Haughey, Bertie Aherne et al.

Frank feels strongly that *Bull Island* had re-established RTÉ's
reputation for satirical TV. It was attracting huge ratings and
when the show ended Frank did not feel it personally, but
believes that political pressure had been brought to bear on its
future. 'I had arrived from Cork that Sunday and got a call at
Dublin Airport inquiring if I was willing to go on Joe Duffy's
Liveline the next day. I asked what was it about, and was told

that *Bull Island* had been axed. I was gutted. I had just bought a house. *Bull Island* was a perfectly good concept. It had an excellent set of actors and writers but, in the end, it was analysed to death.'

The truly great and natural stage performers have an instinct for visual comedy. Charlie Chaplin, Jack Benny and Woody Allen could elicit an unexpected response from an audience; a response which would not seem likely on a simple reading of a script. Nearer home, Frank Duggan has it as Cha. So it was with the late Ignatius Comerford and now his cousin, Paddy.

Frank Twomey and Pakie O'Callaghan in Santa Ponsa or Bust
(© Everyman Palace Theatre)

Frank Twomey also possesses that gift. There was a straightforward scene in the first *Santa Ponsa*, when Frank is laying out some traffic cones. He arranges and rearranges the cones. No need for words, each member of the audience saw the character established and conveyed in those first seconds of silence.

Frank recalls: 'Back in Cork, Pakie O'Callaghan was doing a one-man show in the Everyman Palace. He asked me to do a spot and collaborate on one of the sketches. We were two power walkers and it worked. From that came the idea of the show *Surviving Santa Ponsa*. I'm great at coming up with ideas, but Pakie is the disciplinarian. I find the nine to five aspect of coming up with a show tedious. I rely on Pakie to ensure that we get the show down on paper.'

Two hit shows in the Palace and a tour have brought *Santa Ponsa* around the county. Pakie and Frank are in thoughtful mode, so expect the laughter to fill theatres again. *Bull Island* has sunk without trace, but there could be more troubled waters ahead for the latest generation of movers and shakers.

Chapter 29
A Man for All Reasons

Pat Talbot

So, finally, we come to the man whose idea it was to put on record the achievements of those who create that other world that mirrors reality but does not supplant it.

Pat Talbot is a rare breed of theatre man in that he has been as at home in the wings as centre stage. His present role as Director of the Everyman Palace has revealed not only his administrative capacity, but also his all-encompassing vision for theatre in the Ireland of the twenty-first century.

Take the idea of a theatre venue adopting the role of a co-publishing house; this role, though not new to the theatre in the UK and US, is a rarity in a country that bequeathed O'Casey, Synge, Beckett and Friel to the world. This is changing, thanks to Pat: witness Vera Ryan's wonderfully warm, *Dan Donovan – An Everyman's Life*, an oral memoir of a co-founder of the Everyman Theatre, published by the Everyman Palace and Collins Press. Pat believes that an activity such as in-house publishing is important if a theatre venue is to make a contribution to the community that it serves, and on which it relies for support.

I was curious, then, to know more about this 'man for all reasons'. I wondered how he first became attracted to this somewhat crazy world within a world? What brought him first to a stage door and why he has stayed when others have got 'proper jobs' in commerce, industry, the professions and academia? Shakespeare was not his suit in school, but he has always been attracted to the funny side of life, as portrayed on stage.

Pat is convinced that humour is all about recognition: audiences look up and see something of themselves in the on-stage characters. They see society reflected back at them, even if that on-stage society is a caricature. This is the measure of all successful performing arts. And laughter is the greatest therapy that any of us can have. If theatre is a mirror held up to nature and we can laugh at what we see, then that is an extraordinary combination.

> No matter how sophisticated we become technologically, and no matter how sophisticated young children are now, with all of that, the ability of theatre – and particularly panto – to produce awe and wonder in children is just unique.
>
> It is the power of storytelling: the suspension of disbelief; the complete engagement with narrative; the total immersion of children in slapstick comedy which I experienced as a performer . . . encountering that awe – that joy, on a year in, year out basis – that really does restore your faith in the power of theatre to transport people, if only momentarily.

Pat loved his time in panto. 'The Demon in *Little Red Riding Hood*, the Giant in *Jack and the Beanstalk* and Abanaazar in *Aladdin* – I seemed to rotate those parts over a number of years, under the direction of Michael Twomey.'

Cape Fear: Pat Talbot as Count Dragemov and Noel Barrett as Skelator in a scene from Red Riding Hood

Pat opened his theatrical heart to Everyman Palace audiences when he wrote his 'Giant's Tale', in a programme note to the Catherine Mahon Buckley-directed production of *Jack and the Beanstalk*, 2007–8.

He recalled the two previous occasions when he had been cast as the Giant and had begun to get inside the head of the man whom children love to hate; so much so that they will scream hysterically at him every time he utters the words: 'Fee, Fi, Fo, Fum.'

At 6 foot 6 inches tall Pat is also a giant in real life; on panto stilts he was over 7 foot and an obvious target for the youngsters' boos and hisses. In one memorable scene at the Opera House he burst into song, telling the children that he was the 'Hoochie Coochie' giant and pleaded: 'Do you love me?' He was met by a chorus of over a thousand voices in the Opera House roaring, 'No', they did not! 'Remember we used to do about fifty shows, so that was me having 50,000 people screaming they did not love me over a whole Christmas and New Year.'

Pat was suffering for his art and enjoying every minute of it, though being locked on to stilts and in padded clothing for a few hours every night – matinees too – was tough going. But hardest of all to bear was knowing that nobody really loves a giant.

> One of the reasons for commissioning this book was to mark an era that was no longer there. For generations of people, in much the same way as sport defined what being Cork is all about . . . for many generations the humour as performed by characters in the *Slag* shows . . . the *Swans, Summer Revels, Up Cork!, Artful Dodgers*, characters like Paddy Cotter, Paddy Coughlan, Billa O'Connell, Paddy Comerford, Tony Hegarty, Cha and Miah, et cetera . . . actually defined what being Cork and a Corkonian was all about.
>
> Cha and Miah helped to define Cork character and Cork wit nationally. That type of comedy is of a particular era, and it has not been replaced, but those who were brilliant and unique in doing what they did, had to be acknowledged in this book.

I'm always intrigued as to how people first connect with theatre, and so I put the question to Pat.

Theatre found me. It goes way back to secondary school at Coláiste Chríost Rí. A teacher at the school was John O'Shea, a co-founder of the Everyman Theatre movement. It was the early '70s, when I was in second year Inter Cert, and John taught me English. I think he saw that I had an aptitude or flair for theatre.

I started out as an actor in school plays. Coláiste has produced Sean McCarthy, Dermot Crowley and world-renowned designer, Bob Crowley. John introduced me to the Everyman Playhouse. They had moved from their Castle Street venue at CCYMS around '72 or '73. I became involved in the re-upholstering of seats in the Father Mathew Hall before it opened to become the Playhouse.

This was my introduction to theatre in terms of production, performance and direction of a world repertoire of plays. I met a lot of extraordinary people, such as Michael McCarthy, Michael Twomey, Dan Donovan and others. Formative influences for me then would have been John O'Shea's production of *A Man for All Seasons, Uncle Vanya*, Arthur Miller's *Death of a Salesman* (directed by Michael Twomey, with Dan Donovan and Lorna Daly) . . . Dan Donovan again, as the father in *All My Sons*. These would have been revelatory experiences for me, as they tapped into me as a student, which, at the time, I did not really comprehend.

I was a pathologically shy young man. Theatre opened me up as a social being. It was a channel to the outside world. Theatre was something I did not have to apologise for as an individual. I was a very keen sportsperson. I was active in hurling and gaelic football as a young student. I was not a bad goalkeeper in my time, for the obvious reason of my 6-foot 6-inch height. I was in primary school when Coláiste achieved a double All-Ireland win.

In tandem with Pat's activity with Everyman, he became involved with the Turrett Players who worked out of the Group Theatre in South Main Street.

My first stage experience with Everyman was a Christmas Show called *Humble and Bumble Come to Town*, written and directed by the legendary John Morley. His son, Christopher, was the famous Royal Shakespeare designer. In the cast was a young American, Anthony Shaw.

There was some secrecy about this young man, which did not become apparent until opening night when there was a knock on the dressing room door. The legendary actress Angela Lansbury had come to wish us well. Anthony was her son. She wished us all the very best for the show, put her arms around me and kissed me. I felt I had been anointed.

Anthony went on to head up Corrymore Productions, the company that produced the hit series *Murder She Wrote*, with Angela Lansbury as its star.

I became fascinated, not just with the performing theatre, but the whole backstage scene. I was really curious to know how the whole theatre thing was put together. I now wanted to understand the mechanics of theatre. In that respect the Everyman was a brilliant training ground. They were all hugely talented people and all volunteers.

The resident stage-manager was Gerry Cunningham. Eoin Nolan looked after the lighting and Don Kelly was on sound. Frank Fitzgerald was into set design and it was here that I got to know Bob Crowley, now a multi Tony Award winner as one of the best theatre designers in the world.

Pat recalls that he encountered Bob first as a performer. The Everyman Playhouse staged a revue called *Party Pieces*, which was quite an irreverent revue, written by Peter Bell, then theatre manager. Bob did some great parodies and accompanied himself on guitar. Those sketches also featured Gerry McLoughlin, Ber Power and Sue Milch. 'I headed for UCC and within a year I left. College was not a good experience for me as I spent most of my time at the Everyman Playhouse, though those around me had advised me to focus on my studies. I was not listening.'

Out of college, where the great Fifi Wilson was completing her studies before embarking on her incredible career as Fiona Shaw, Pat began his work with Irish National Ballet as assistant stage-manager. Donn McMullin was general manager and Donn would go on to a very long and successful career with Everyman. 'I was promoted to stage-manager and it was an amazing experience with Joan Denis Moriarty as artistic director.'

I can quite understand Pat's enthusiasm in the presence of the 'First Lady of Dance'. I once witnessed a combination of the exquisite athleticism of ballet and the power of Irish music, fused for Synge's classic *The Playboy of the Western World* at the Opera House in Cork, before its world tour in 1979. Accompaniment was by the brilliant Chieftains – and it was a triumph for Joan Denise and her brave company, Irish Ballet, presented by Noel Pearson. It created that kind of stir with the public which would be achieved by *Riverdance* years later. Design was by Pat Murray.

Pat Talbot was fascinated by stage management, but Joan Denise had another unlikely role for him. This lady of stately frame once chose Pat to be her partner when she wished to demonstrate a particular dance movement at rehearsal.

> It was quite a special experience, dancing with Joan Denise. I have a sense of movement and rhythm, but I'm not good at counting time. I got a job with Scottish Ballet just before the *Playboy* opened, so I missed the première performances, but I was with them for its international tour, which was in Yugoslavia in the late '70s, and also for its first visit to Northern Ireland.
>
> I came back from Scotland after two years and joined the Cork Theatre Company, which was then a fledgling company run by Gerry Barnes, with Maurice O'Donoghue, Ger FitzGibbon and Fred Williams. I was actor-cum-stage-manager, cum production manager. It was a collective of about seven people who aspired to be members of a fully professional company based in Cork.

I also reconnected with Everyman and it was at this time that I directed and designed my first full-length play, *One for the Road*, which featured Pakie O'Callaghan and Anne Shanahan, now a script editor with *Fair City*. It also starred Melody McNamara and Gerry Motherway. It is an hilarious rite-of-passage play, as a man facing his fortieth birthday ruminates on the middle-age crisis. I also did a Christmas production of *Pinocchio* for Everyman, while still working with CTC.

When I was away from home in Glasgow, and in a job which was not working out, I was too inexperienced and too young. I was looking after Scottish Ballet's touring and education units and it was too much responsibility for me. One way of dealing with it was to drink more than I should. I became a denizen of a great number of pubs on the Great Western Road in Glasgow. I left Glasgow to try and escape the awful reality of life for me at that time.

In Cork I was working away, but as the '80s progressed my life became more and more chaotic to the point where it completely broke down in '87. After a spell it was essentially like starting all over again. It took me two or three years to get a sense of who I was, where I was, and where I was headed.

Liz Cooper and Pat started Feedback Theatre Company with the aim of providing Cork with a viable and enduring theatre entity that would offer full and meaningful employment to local artistes and technicians. For Pat personally, Feedback was an attempt to make up for lost time. He harnessed his excess energy to produce a succession of high standard productions, including: Tom Murphy's *Conversations on a Homecoming*; Michael Harding's *Una Pooka*; *Factory Girls* by Frank McGuinness; and *Juno and the Paycock* by O'Casey at the new Everyman Palace. The latter had a powerful cast, including Dan Coughlan, Paddy Comerford and Gerry McLoughlin. Odd play out from that Irish repertoire was another production of *One for the Road*, this time with Joe Stockdale, Joe O'Gorman, Martina Carroll and Ashley Buckle.

The late '80s was not a good time for theatre in Cork, with the closure of CTC and the end of the Ivernia Theatre as a venue.

> We had lost the Irish National Ballet. The Everyman Playhouse had closed at Father Mathew Hall for the move to the Palace in MacCurtain Street and an opening in 1990. Even the Opera House was going through a shaky patch.
>
> It was a very bleak time. There were no employment opportunities, so Liz Cooper and I were keen to remain on in Cork to express ourselves through the theatre. We formed our own company with the invaluable assistance of FÁS and a community employment scheme. A lot of arts activity here and elsewhere relied heavily on the support of FÁS. We quickly forget just how awful things were in those days. There was very little public money coming through the Arts Council, so a lot of companies subsisted through FÁS.

Pat was happy with his direction of Michael Harding's *Una*

Pooka in the Triskel. There was also *A View from the Bridge* by Arthur Miller, designed memorably with a Brooklyn Bridge motif by Pat Murray in the small performance space. Liz Cooper did a wonderful *Conversations on a Homecoming* and Pat Kiernan directed Tom Kilroy's *Talbot's Box*, which played the Triskel and the Project Arts Centre in Dublin.

Inevitably, Pat would burn out again. This time from the sheer workload. 'We got our first Arts Council grant in 1994, which was the year we did *Talbot's Box*. I was exhausted and depressed, losing all confidence and self-esteem. I turned down the funding for the Council for 1995.'

Feedback produced plays from 1991 to 1996, although it was involved in co-productions with the Everyman Palace up to 1998. Pat would soon get back his sense of direction when he got a phone call from the Gate Theatre to ask if he would take over the production department.

> I had a fantastic three years at the Gate. It was a hectic period for the theatre. It was dominated by the Pinter Festival in New York, which the Gate curated, where we had over fourteen plays in a period of two weeks to mark the playwright's seventieth birthday. I spent about six months organising this festival at the Lincoln Centre. It was in association with the Royal Court and Almeida Theatres in London. Featured actors included Ian Holm and Penelope Wilton. Karl Reitz came to direct. It was a special time and the icing on the cake was that Harold Pinter himself directed *The Room* and *Celebration* and also appeared in *One for the Road*.
>
> In the Gate I met Neil Labute and that working

friendship led to the Everyman Palace premièring his *Wrecks*, starring Ed Harris, in 2005. At the Gate I also worked on the world première of *Port Authority* and on the Irish première of *Dublin Carol*, which I subsequently directed at the Palace.

Three years into my stint at the Gate, the Everyman job came up and here I am. One of the first things I did was to ask Neil Labute to write a play.

Pat Talbot is so busy with developing the artistic role of the Everyman Palace that he has little time to look back on the road he has so far travelled. But he does pay tribute to those who have made an impression on him, particularly in the context of comedy theatre in his native city.

Summer Revels had a good share of working class humour – raw Cork humour which unashamedly celebrated the traditional Cork character, rogue or villain . . . usually under pressure to find a job, or avoid a job, or escape a tyrannical wife. The writing was razor-sharp. The duo Cha and Miah was a brilliant creation, with their hilarious political and social satire. The simple setting of a bar was the perfect forum for their prognostications on life, with the passive, deadpan-faced barman [Dick Healy] doling out the libations. Cha and Miah in many respects defined the working class Cork 'character' for the nation.

One of the hallmarks of *Revels* was the ensemble playing and the extraordinary rapport between the principals: in particular Billa O'Connell, Paddy Comerford, Michael Twomey, Frank Duggan, and later Noel Barrett and Pat Sullivan of *Swans* fame. I firmly believe that if they had been born and lived in the US or the UK they would have become international comedy stars.

One of the funniest sketches ever played on the Opera House stage, or on any other stage in Cork, was the 'Big Hole' sketch, which involved the entire *Revels* team. This was simply a study of the eternity it took for a bunch of workers to dig a hole in the city street. Written by Michael Twomey, I can still hear the uncontrollable laughter of audiences night after night. Those audiences looked up at the stage and saw exaggerated versions of themselves and their city.

In the three decades that I have been active in theatre in Cork, there is no doubt that the main driving force behind stage comedy has been Michael Twomey. While his contribution to drama is well recorded, his contribution to stage comedy is less so, in my view. As a scriptwriter, performer, director and broadcaster, he has been the link between *Slags*, *Summer Revels*, Cha and Miah, *Jury's Cabaret* and countless pantomimes in the Opera House and the Everyman Palace. Michael has an innate under-standing of the workings of comedy in respect of the structure of a comedy routine or sketch. These include the delivery of a gag, the delicacies of timing and pace, et cetera. Performers like Billa and Paddy Comerford have relied on him hugely in this respect. They will be the first to pay tribute to his talents as a writer and director of comedy. Michael is a rare all-rounder. I was very fortunate to be directed by him in many pantos in the Opera House and all through the '90s.

Pat Talbot was a stage-hand in the Opera House in the 1980s when *Summer Revels*, the big revue show, was packing them into the big theatre. He maintains that Billa O'Connell is to panto and comedy what Roy Keane is to soccer. 'I have never experienced a performer with such energy, enthusiasm and zest for the stage. He is a life-force and this force rubs off when you work on stage with him. He inhabits each and every moment on the stage as if it is his last. Respect for the audience is always paramount for Billa, be it a little toddler, or a grandmother.'

My own fondest memory of Billa is not, curiously enough, his brilliant portrayals of the dame, but rather when he teamed up with Paddy Comerford to form the bewitching Ugly Sisters in a version of *Cinderella* at the Opera House. This pairing worked because their approach to comic creation came from different directions and, as a combined force, they were incomparable.

Pat Talbot considers Paddy Comerford as the great stylist.

Paddy works in miniature with all of his characterisations, like pencil sketches. He is a Dick Van Dyke crossed with Fred Astaire. His Uncle Peter is a ribald celebration of old age, while his Simple Simon in various pantos, had such an innate understanding of childish fun that kids in the audience could never get enough of him. He was *them* up on stage. His twenty-minute appearance during the 'Remembering Pat Murray' Gala Night in 2007 was a brilliant star-turn which evoked a whole era of comedy in Cork.

Noel Barrett and Pat Sullivan are, for Pat Talbot, the quintessential comedy act and one of the most original of its kind in the country. This duo came from the great *Swans* era when master-class givers were Paddy Cotter, Tommy Dynes, Paddy Coughlan and Bill Mahony, taking off with a brilliant Paudie Harris script.

> The slapstick comedy of Noel Barrett and Pat Sullivan goes right back to the music hall and variety days of Fred Karno and Charlie Chaplin. They are the natural descendents of Laurel and Hardy. Their mimes are legendary, but even in straight comedy routines they define themselves not just in terms of straight man/funny man, but also with their physicality. Pat Sullivan, being taller, is elegant and graceful and his finger-pointing gestures add great texture to the script, while Noel Barrett makes a virtue of being shorter and slightly more rotund, even though he actually isn't. His flailing with his arms as the funny man is sometimes an hilarious counter-point to the precision gestures of Pat Sullivan.

Pat Talbot may be lost in admiration for the undoubted talents of those he has met on life's journey so far – but he himself has, in a real sense, evolved into an 'everyman' of theatre. By 2008, he had established the Everyman Palace as the leading venue in the country for touring companies and an invaluable platform for locally produced theatre. It was particularly fitting that his own play, *Rita Dunne*, was staged at the Palace in 2008.

His has been a real pilgrim's progression, from stage door to front of house – sometimes exhausting and helter-skelter, yet always exhilarating – a roller-coaster ride through life. He has been the wide-eyed student and fan, stage-hand, performer, director, producer, respected manager, now writer; all in a business which can tax, consume, exasperate and enrich those who encounter its sheer magicality.

Afterword
Raise a Toast

Raise a glass of kindness and warmth in remembrance of present and absent friends who have lit up our little lives with their brilliance.

The manic world of staging a show is only possible with the support of so many people who may not even get a programme note. It is they who ensure that all is well on the night.

Do the benign spirits of many of these dedicated people from Cork's theatre past – now sadly lost to us – flit, hover between the tabs, as fly ropes sway, tremble, guided by unseen hands beside the darkened stage?

Backstage is that world where real life's own dramas are forgotten, because now the show is the thing for those in love with the very act of theatre itself. Then the curtain closes, midnight approaches, the stage door is slammed shut, the empty building cocoons, wraps, keeps safe the tears, the laughter, awaiting another time when the call is to 'light the lights', as the carousel of live performance begins to revolve once more. *Make 'Em Laugh!* is dedicated to all those whose God-given talents help us to see the funny side of life.

Curtain! House lights!

Index

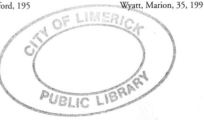